THE GOOD NEWS
IS
JESUS

Kilian McGowan, C.P.

THE SIGN PRESS
Monastery Place
Union City, N.J.

THE SIGN PRESS
Monastery Place
Union City, New Jersey 07087

© 1981 by Passionist Missions, Inc.
All rights reserved.
First edition

Imprimi potest: The Very Rev. Brendan Keevey, C.P.
　　　　　　　　　Provincial, St. Paul of the Cross Province

Nihil obstat: The Very Rev. Victor Hoagland, C.P.
　　　　　　　Censor librorum

Imprimatur: † Peter L. Gerety
　　　　　　　Most Rev. Peter L. Gerety, D.D.
　　　　　　　Archbishop of Newark

ISBN 0-938892-00-2

Second printing

Printed in the United States of America.

Introduction

This book was written to help the sincere follower of Jesus Christ today to reflect on the key areas of his or her relationship with the Lord. It is based on the assumption that as our imitation of Christ Jesus progresses, we will be more and more compelled to spread the Good News of the Gospel. Because modern men and women are more impressed by witnesses than by teachers, today's disciples of Jesus Christ will, above all, evangelize the world by their evident faithfulness to the Lord Jesus and his Gospel.

Our approach flows from the belief that God engages in constant communication with his people. One of the signs of our times through which God has spoken is, I believe, the Apostolic Exhortation on Evangelization of the late Pope Paul VI. In this exhortation the Holy Father insisted that we must internalize the Gospel message by our own conversion and inner renewal before we can hope to join his mission in spreading the Good News.

The chapters of this book are intended to indicate the kind of conversion and inner renewal that is needed for any Christian anxious to share the precious gift he or she has received in Jesus Christ. The exhortation on evangelization clearly states that there is no evangelization if the name, the teachings, the life, the promises, the kingdom, and the mystery of Jesus Christ are not proclaimed. It is the author's cherished hope that this small book may be a guide to inner renewal for the reader and, even more, may prod him or her to proclaim that THE GOOD NEWS IS JESUS!

TABLE OF CONTENTS

CHAPTER I

This Person Called Jesus

In the opening lines of his first encyclical, the recently installed Pope John Paul II wrote that Jesus is the center of the human race and history. Words of a papal encyclical, even the wisest and most inspirational, are meaningless unless somehow we internalize them and make them words that we truly live by. And so, the question for each of us to ponder and to answer becomes something like this: "Is Jesus Christ the center of my human history?" or "In what way has his life honestly affected mine?"

He asks each one of us the key question put to the disciples in Luke 9:20: "What about YOU: Who do YOU say that I am?"

If the good God has intended that our life be truly centered on Christ, if he has predestined us to a deep personal relationship with him, doesn't it make sense for each of us to evaluate that relationship at each stage of the journey of life? Or is it possible that there is not enough in our life to witness to the truth that he actually once walked this earth?

HIS HUMAN BEGINNINGS

History confirms that Jesus appeared on this earth in a definite place at a certain time. He was born somewhere between 7 and 4 B.C. and he died some thirty years later. Unlike the pagan gods, such as Zeus, Diana, or Astarte, he lived on this earth, as did Lincoln, Aristotle, and Caesar. He was born of a human mother in the land of Palestine at a given moment of history. He ate and slept, he worked and prayed, he suffered and he died. Although countless efforts have been made for twenty centuries to reduce him to a mythical figure, it is downright unreasonable for an objective person to doubt his human existence.

There is no mystery clouding the human origins of Jesus. A descendant of David, the warrior-king of Israel, he was born in Bethlehem and raised in Nazareth of Galilee. His birth was ordinary in itself, although extraordinary happenings were reported as having taken place on this great event. Except for a

few events, we know very little about the next
quarter century of his life.

THE BACKGROUND OF JESUS

Jesus was a Galilean artisan . . . the foster son
of a carpenter. His contemporaries expected
him to act as carpenter, and not as a messianic
rabbi. They asked: "From where does he get
this wisdom? How can he speak with such
authority? How can he work such wonders?"

Nothing good was supposed to come from
the obscure village of a culturally backward
province. At the Temple in Jerusalem he was
no different from any simple pilgrim. He held
no official position and was a leader in none of
its prayers or worship.

Jesus did come from a specific Jewish culture
and he did have a well-structured religious
background. Later, he would challenge the
religious leaders in the motivations of their worship of God and their interpretations of God's
law.

He must have been profoundly conscious of
his formation as a Jew. Being immersed in a
biblical culture, he shared a knowledge of the
history of salvation as communicated to him by
his parents and teachers. He had a deep em-

pathy for the desires of his people for the coming of the Messiah and of their awareness of having a special place in the history of salvation.

BEGINNING OF HIS MISSION

When he first began to preach, his audiences noted nothing extraordinary about him. Reflect on this: for almost 90 percent of his life he lived and acted as a foster son of a humble carpenter in a small village in a looked-down-upon province. Suddenly, with no advance warning of any kind, he began to speak with such wisdom and authority that people were surprised and shocked. When he first began to speak of his mission, they expelled him from the synagogue. Even his relatives "set out to take charge of him, convinced he was out of his mind." Only later, when they began to share in his fame, were they happy to see the world flock to him.

Attuned as we are to such dramatic presentations of the life of Jesus as Zeffirelli's *Jesus of Nazareth* or *Jesus Christ, Superstar,* we can easily overlook the humanness of the greater portion of his earthly career.

We shouldn't be too hard on his listeners in those first days; we might have been no different. We forget too easily that we look at Jesus through the knowledge of his Resurrection-triumph over sin and death and comforted by the survival of Christianity for two thousand years.

Why should we be spared the struggle to understand the most unusual man in all of history? God had his reasons for clothing the person of Jesus in such mystery. We are companions with Jesus on a long journey; maybe God wishes to make this journey of understanding a gradual and growing one.

Once his public career began, Jesus seemed to be completely absorbed in his mission. There was a consistent singleheartedness about him. It almost seemed as though his family ceased to exist. Or it might be more true to say that he acted as though the whole world were his family: "Here are my brothers and sisters. Anyone who does the will of God is my brother and sister and mother."

No longer did he belong to himself. And he expected the same of his disciples: "Any one who prefers father or mother to me is not worthy of me." He never seemed to show undue favor to members of his family or to relatives or friends. Never attached to any one place, he was ever on the move: "I must preach there too."

He was rarely physically alone, except during his hours of prayer alone with his Father in the desert or on the mountaintop. He moved easily and comfortably from the demands of one moment to those of the next and didn't seem to have a super-organized set of plans.

He never preached in secret. Available to everyone from the beginning of his preaching career, he treated each with a singular reverence and kindness. His healing power constantly went out to their illnesses of mind, heart, and body.

His mission absorbed him totally. The spirit of the Lord had taken over in him. Yet, through it all, he was perfectly human.

THE DISCIPLES OF JESUS

Jesus was aware that his relationship with his apostles, as with us, is based on his unique selection of each of them: "You have not chosen me, but I have chosen you." This relationship flowed from their election to share his mission. Shortly after he called them, he sent them out in pairs to preach the Good News, also giving them power to work wonders and cast out unclean spirits.

Like ourselves, they were slow to understand Jesus or his real mission. Despite this difficulty in understanding him, however, they did love him. Eventually they believed completely and went forth to the four corners of the world to share that belief.

The concept of a suffering Messiah was alien to them and a scandal to their immature faith. Only gradually and with much patience did Jesus reveal what the Father's will demanded of him. How compassionate he had to be in facing the knowledge that in the hour of his greatest need, their commitment to him would collapse. Except for John, his mother, and a few others, his followers failed to offer him the comfort of their presence and support when, in human terms, he needed them most!

Yet they did truly love him. They were happy when he said, "I have called you friends." And even though they failed the test, they were sincere when they said that they wanted to go and die with him.

THE TRUE IDENTITY OF JESUS

So far, we have seen that historical research has established the approximate date of the birth of Jesus, his human origins and cultural background, and his preaching and his first disciples.

None of these facts explain the unparalleled influence of this man on the course of human history. None explain why almost a billion people claim him as their Lord. None explain why tens of thousands of books have been written about him through the ages.

In human history he stands out as totally unique. There is simply no other person to whom he can be compared. And everyone who writes about him must experience a terrible feeling of inadequacy.

But one thing we can do. We can let him reveal the secret of his own person, for he alone can tell us who he really is. He alone can tell us what human life is all about.

Let us permit Jesus to speak for himself:

I am the Light of the World. I am a King.

I am the Good Shepherd. I am the True Vine.

I am the Resurrection and the Life.

I am the Bread of Life that comes down from Heaven.

I am the Way, the Truth, and the Life!

These statements alone, from all he has said, tell us a great deal about Jesus of Nazareth.

Questions to Ask Yourself

1. Do you really know this man called Jesus Christ?

2. Exactly what does he mean to you now?

3. Do his person and his life honestly affect your daily life? How?

4. Have you really tried to internalize his message and make it your own?

5. Are you willing to surrender your life into his hands with complete trust and confidence?

6. How often do you stop and ask: "Lord, what would you have me to do?"

7. What, in terms of friendship and love, is your present relationship to Jesus?

Words to Remember

"Are you 'He who is to come,' or do we look for someone else?" (At that time he was curing many of their diseases, afflictions, and evil spirits; he also restored sight to many who were blind.)

Jesus gave us this response: Go and report to John what you have seen and heard:

The blind recover their sight, cripples walk, lepers are cured, the deaf hear, dead men are raised to life and the poor have the good news preached to them.

Blest is that man who finds no stumbling block in me.

(Luke 7:20–23)

CHAPTER II

Be Changed in Your Heart

When driving along the highway, I frequently turn on a religious program. I like to listen to different preachers' interpretations of various sections of the Bible. Especially, I look for his or her insights into the call of the Lord for conversion.

The very first words that Jesus uttered in St. Mark's Gospel dealt with this urgent topic:

Jesus appeared in Galilee proclaiming the good news of God: "This is the time of fulfillment. The reign of God is at hand! Reform your lives and believe in the gospel!"

(Mark 1:14–15)

Mark said a remarkable amount in two verses, to say nothing of the balance he achieved in so few words—a balance all too often missed by preachers of the Word. First of all, he states that the "news" is good, not threatening; the "time" is one of fulfillment and not of disaster; God's reign of justice and peace is forthcoming; and finally, reform and don't despair of your life no matter what it has been up to this moment.

The "Good News" is the revelation that in the fullness of time, a loving God sent his beloved Son to invite each one of us to share the intimacy of the family of God. He offers each one an opportunity to be refashioned in the likeness of Jesus, who is to become our Way, our Truth, and our Life.

It is "the time of fulfillment" because Jesus has invited us to his Father's house. He himself will establish the reign of his Father within our hearts and lives. He wishes to share every moment of our lives. He will mold our hearts and desires by sending his Spirit, whose healing love will make all things new.

The word that Mark uses to say "Reform your lives" is *metanoia*, which has been translated as "Be changed in your heart!" This means that Jesus asks for a conversion that calls for a complete change of heart. This change will reach gradually into the innermost core of self from which proceed all desires, motivations, and outward expressions of one's needs and personality.

When Jesus says, "Believe in the Gospel," he is promising you a renewed vision of life. Whether consciously or not, each. of us operates out of a certain vision of life that we have adopted as our very own. This vision embraces the attitudes and instincts, goals and values underlying every single activity of our lives. Jesus knows that the light of his Gospel will in time completely refashion this vision of life, penetrating it with the light of God.

Before going any further, let us state that **authentic conversion at its inner levels should always be a sincere response to the person and the love of Jesus Christ**. He IS the Good News —the gift of God par excellence! And, in the normal process of human growth that we call life, each ongoing conversion implies an ever-deepening blending of our lives with his. He has come that we "might have life and have it more abundantly," and that life is his!

THE INVITATION TO PERFECTION

Our Lord's call to "Be perfect as your Heavenly Father is perfect" can be rather unnerving to one all too conscious of his or her failures and weaknesses. We must remember

that he presents this ideal as the goal of a
lifetime. We must not be discouraged if our
progress seems to be lackluster, or even if we
appear to be backsliding. A study of the Gospel
pages will show that Jesus never demanded success in our efforts, even though he never ex-
cused us from trying.

An ongoing effort to achieve increasing
faithfulness to the will of the Lord is indeed
success. Remember his kindly and forgiving patience with the slow progress and the frequent
misunderstandings of his first disciples. Only
after his death did the Spirit of the Lord take
command of their lives. Even then they had a
lot of growing to do.

The truth appears to be that Jesus is more
aware of our unique goodness than of our quite
evident weaknesses. He issues the call for a
complete conversion because he has promised
—and he is ever faithful to these promises—to
give us a new heart and a new spirit, but only in
his time, not ours. This may be the most difficult lesson of all to learn.

Our Lord only once in the entire Gospel gave
a concrete model for conversion, and that was a
little child. When his apostles were fighting
over who should have the "highest place" in
heaven he cautioned them:

Unless you become converted and become as little children, You shall not enter the Kingdom of Heaven.

A child has a simple trust and a total confidence in its father, just as we should with Abba, our heavenly Father.

My personal belief is that most of us achieve the perfect surrender of our lives to the love and will of God only in our last moments on earth. And that also is a gift—the greatest of them all!

BEGINNINGS OF A NEW LIFE

I've met very few people who wouldn't love to be refashioned by a God of love. All too many seem to be totally dissatisfied with themselves. They need reassurance that they can become new persons by being transformed from above, or even more precisely from within, where the healing love of the Savior goes to work. They will discover that wholehearted devotion to Christ causes an inner transformation that remakes one's personality. Rarely does it happen in the twinkling of an eye, but rather by stumbling steps and painstaking efforts. And that very effort is success!

Our generation is characterized by its self-consciousness, and pride in its own uniqueness, and need for personal self-fulfillment. So let us clearly affirm that it's never necessary to renounce a single ounce of our personal goodness. Our Lord wants us to rid ourselves only of what is not truly ourselves—whatever is inhuman or selfish—whatever places a barrier to his healing care and loving action within ourselves. The call of Christ is truly glad tidings of great joy to all his people. We are invited by the good God to become that unique individual he has eternally intended. He has come that we might have life and have it more abundantly!

THE STAGES OF CONVERSION

To accept the loving invitation of God to become new persons in Christ, we need the following dispositions:

Be conscious that the time of fulfillment is NOW.
    Be disposed to open your mind to the Good News of the Lord and open your heart to the unbelievable joy of receiving his healing and uplifting love.

Respond to the call of Christ. Believe that conversion is fundamentally a humble and sincere response to the person of Jesus and the love of God as seen in Jesus.

Pray for a loving heart. The signs of the presence of the spirit of Jesus will be obvious in your life. Offer yourself to the Lord just as you are at this moment. Be willing to let him change you in his way and at his time.

Accept the responsibility for your sins and mistakes. Do this as a means of facing yourself as you are, but coupled with a growing trust in him who said that he wouldn't harm the "bruised reed" or the "smoking flax."

Remember that he is the Potter and you are the clay. Show him you really trust him by placing yourself daily in his hands, to refashion, to heal, to love, to make truly beautiful!

Questions to Ask Yourself

1. Do you really understand the Lord's invitation to "Come, follow me" or to be "perfect as your Heavenly Father is perfect"?

2. Are you willing to look deeply into your human heart with all its motivations and let the Lord help you achieve an inner change?

3. Do you really believe that you can become a totally new person in Christ? Do you want this to happen?

4. Do you now understand that conversion is an ongoing daily response to the person of Jesus and the love of God?

5. What, if anything, is holding you back?

Words to Remember

Praised be the God and Father of our Lord Jesus Christ, who has bestowed on us in Christ every spiritual blessing in the heavens!

God chose us in him before the world began, to be holy and blameless in his sight, to be full of love.

He likewise predestined us through Jesus Christ to be his adopted sons [and daughters]—such was his will and pleasure— that all might praise the glorious favor he has bestowed on us in his beloved.

(Eph. 1:3–6)

CHAPTER III

Searching for the Real Jesus

In early 1980, a film was released and promoted called *In Search of the Historical Jesus*. A major portion of the film is dedicated to consideration of the authenticity of the Shroud of Turin, reputed to be the burial cloth of Jesus after his Crucifixion and death. First reports indicate that the group of forty scientists who carefully examined this shroud over a period of months favored a declaration of its authenticity. Some, indeed, have already published their belief that the shroud is truly the cloth in which Jesus was buried.

Isn't it true that the life of each Christian is a search for the real Jesus? And isn't the heart of the Good News the unbelievable gift that God has given us in the fullness of time—that gift we call Jesus Christ? In a very real sense, the life story of each Christian is a historical record of a personal relationship with Jesus—and, through him, with the Father and the Holy Spirit.

The insistent call to conversion with which Jesus opened his preaching campaign is an invitation to be changed in our hearts as well as an invitation to permit the Lord's Spirit to refashion us from within.

We heed the urgent call of Jesus to "Come, follow me" when we take the first steps, no matter how insecure or stumbling, in his direction. We start off simply by listening to him, by studying his words and works, by letting him speak to our hearts. We really need only take the first step and trust that the Lord will lead us from stage to stage in the journey of faith.

Regardless of our age or condition, we can all become new persons in Christ. Probably, all we need at the beginning is the readiness to let him make us over. Only by degrees will he reorient our lives and recreate our value system. He will in time give us a renewed vision of life, as the light of the Gospel dispels the inner darkness of our spirit. He knows that we are all inclined, at first, to fight the light; so he will heal as he enlightens.

THE REAL MEANING OF LIFE

What we are really trying to say is that the only real meaning of life is union with Jesus Christ in humble and self-sacrificing love. He should become as real to us as what we daily see and hear and touch. This calls for a daily self-emptying, a daily laying down of our lives in things great and small, which is really our reliving of the Paschal Mystery of Jesus. The healing love of Jesus will empower us to empty our hearts of all that is not loved in God, for God, and through God. His indwelling Spirit will so activate our desires as to enable us to state with St. Paul: "I live, now it is no longer I, but it is Christ who lives in me."

If this ideal seems to be utterly beyond the reach of the ordinary follower of Christ, be assured that Jesus wishes to play an active part in the project of developing a Christlike character. We should not fear that we may have to go it alone because an essential part of the divine plan is the revealed desire of the Lord to share in every moment and every activity of our lives. He is far more anxious than we are to share a deep and intimate relationship. The Apostle Paul reminds us of this inspiring truth again and again, and gave unmistakable witness to it by his apostolic life.

Baptism is the beginning of this lifetime partnership; the complete transformation into Christ is the work of a lifetime. Unbelievable as it may seem, Christ is anxious to become our other self. He who lived his life for you now wishes to relive it in you. The ultimate proof of this is the Eucharist, wherein he makes a total presentation of everything he is and has done for you.

A MODEL FOR CONVERSION TO CHRIST

A delightfully human account of the conversion of some of the first disciples is found in John 1:35–39. The conversion-story of two of the followers of John the Baptist is recorded. One, according to the Gospel, was Andrew, while the other disciple, according to tradition, was John himself.

The account tells us that one day as the two were listening to John on the banks of the Jordan, a stranger walked by. The Baptist immediately said: "Look, there is the Lamb of God." Hearing this, the two disciples of John followed Jesus—for he was the stranger. Turning around and seeing them, Jesus asked: "What are you looking for?" They answered with another question: "Teacher, where do you stay?" He invited them to find out: "Come and see!" Whereupon, they went with him to his lodging and spent the rest of the day with him. John's

Gospel tells us no more about what happened after that late afternoon meeting.

Did Andrew and John know at that time what "the Lamb of God" meant? Did they dare to think that he might be the Messiah? Even God's eternal Son? Probably all they knew was the he was a teacher who spoke the words of God. But undoubtedly they experienced an irresistible attraction, something they had never experienced before. They simply had to go and see what he was like. They responded to the interior call of grace with their first faltering steps after the Master. Had they not done so, we would not today call them "apostles."

We can learn a great deal from this account of the first stages of the conversion of Andrew and John. After their discovery of Christ, they did something about it. Too many today will be touched by an account of the life of Jesus, such as Zeffirelli's *Jesus of Nazareth*, and then return to a life-as-usual pattern. The disciples were attracted by the person of Jesus and did something about it—they went to see who he was and what he was about. They spent the remainder of that day, and many more, with him.

A great lesson flows from this incident. Once we have discovered Jesus Christ, we must be willing to "spend time" with him. This is an essential characteristic of every true follower of the Lord, not only at the first stages of one's conversion, but at every stage in the journey of faith. Throughout our lives God will give an unending series of invitations, but he never draws us against our will.

THE FOLLOW-UP TO ONE'S CONVERSION

Think of all that must have happened between the first meeting of John the Apostle and Jesus and the time, perhaps a half-century later, when he wrote: "Eternal life is this: to know you, the only true God, and him whom you have sent, Jesus Christ." (John 17:3) At the latter time, speaking from his experience, John was profoundly convinced that all our progress in the Christian endeavor must be measured by our increasing knowledge, love, and imitation of Jesus. John, as well as the Apostle Paul, would certainly agree that conversion is more a "putting on of Christ" than a dying to sin and selfishness, even though the two are, in reality, inseparable.

Ongoing conversion, therefore, would seem to demand the following elements:

An ever-present willingness to "spend time"

with Jesus, to consciously and consistently make him the chief study of our lives.

To respond generously to his revelation of the mystery of God and the love of the Father for us. A spiritual life based solidly on a deep awareness of Jesus' undying love for us is more likely to avoid a false asceticism and an excessive zeal.

Frequent prayerful reflection on the person and the words of Jesus; and as intimate communication progresses, the development of heart to heart prayer with him.

Imitation of him by internalizing his attitudes and desires, his activities and life motivation, and especially to study prayerfully and imitate the way he relates to each person who touches his life.

An appreciation of the principle of spiritual growth: Jesus loves and accepts us as we are at this moment and not as we wish to be. We simply must start each day where we are, leaving the past to the mercy of God and responding to his daily revelation of himself. If we respond to the leadership of the Spirit, he will surely lead us from grace to grace and to an ever-deepening love of God and humankind.

Finally, taking a cue from the Apostle Paul, we must not be discouraged by our obvious weaknesses, or even our past mistakes. Paul clearly states that we must glory in our weakness so that the power of Christ might dwell in us. We must daily live in an awareness that with Christ we can do all things, just as without him we can do nothing!

Questions to Ask Yourself

1. How frequently do you spend time with Jesus: each day? each week? each month?

2. Honestly reflecting on your own desires have you ever compared them to those of Christ?

3. Have you ever made the Great Decision to dedicate yourself and your life to following Jesus Christ?

4. Do you consistently study and prayerfully reflect on the Gospel portrait of Jesus?

5. What do you believe is the main obstacle to the generous following of Christ in your life? Are you willing to submit this to the healing grace of the Lord?

Words to Remember

This is what we proclaim to you: what was from the beginning, what we have heard, what we have seen with our eyes, what we have looked upon and our hands have touched—we speak of the word of life.

What we have seen and heard we proclaim in turn to you so that you may share life with us. This fellowship of ours is with the Father and with his Son, Jesus Christ.

(1 John 1:1, 3)

CHAPTER IV

The Signs of a Disciple
of Christ

In recent years there has been a great deal of reflection and writing on the meaning of discipleship. In certain dioceses entire renewal programs for the laity have been based on and inspired by this concept. With a deepened awareness of their call to share in the mission of Jesus, and with an increased sharing in the various ministries of the church, the people of God have been asking just what it means to be a disciple of Jesus Christ today.

We are too prone to forget that the first disciples of Jesus will forever be our models in spirituality. Not that they are the only ones, but they are the ones taught and formed by our Lord himself. I recall that I had never seriously considered the apostles as models of spirituality until I read a small but very provocative book by the late Father Garrigou-Lagrange. The book was titled *The Three Ages of the Interior Life*.

The author outlined the three stages of the spiritual life as beginners; those making progress, or progressives; and the perfect, or those under the habitual influence of the Spirit of the Lord. He then discussed the characteristics of each stage and how each was verified in the life of the apostles. He also showed the various conversions that are necessary if the Christian is to continue to grow in the journey of faith.

Father Garrigou-Lagrange taught not only that the apostles are models for our spirituality today, but also that we must experience the same stages of spiritual growth that they did. With this in mind, let us reflect on some essential characteristics of their relationship with the Lord.

A PERSONAL RELATIONSHIP WITH JESUS

At a deeper and more interior level the history of Christianity is but a record of the relationships of the first disciples and each of us with the Lord Jesus and the members of his church—the people of God.

This relationship for each of us may be said to have begun when we were "born" in the mind of God under the impetus of an infinite impulse of divine love. If we are intent on tracing our roots, we must believe that we were conceived in love, called to live in the love of God, and predestined to share it forever. This truth is fundamental to our consciousness of our self-worth.

Our Blessed Lord offered his followers, then and now, a new way to happiness and peace here and hereafter. His value system, as expressed in the Beatitudes, transcends all previous systems of ethics and morality. He made promises that no other person has dared to make. He worked wonders and gave signs of power as yet unseen by humans. He gave meaning to human life and offered answers to the deepest problems of human existence. He invited all to be perfect as his heavenly Father is perfect, but also demanded a definite "Yes" or "No" to the invitation to join him in the mission given him by his Father in heaven.

And how did the disciples respond to this call? First, they looked upon him. They listened to him even when they did not understand him, as when he insisted upon the necessity of his suffering and death. They studied him and spent time with him in a very human way. They had—as must we have—a personal experience of him. Their first conversion was, above all, a response to the person and the words of Jesus.

They knew that not only did he speak as no other man ever spoke, but also that they had never witnessed such goodness before.

We are told that the people of God are formed by the Word of God, and he is "The Word"—the Good News par excellence!

A PROFOUND COMMITMENT TO THE LORD

After heeding the call of Christ, the disciples, by a deliberate decision, completely changed the course of their lives. After the Ascension of our Lord, the Holy Spirit at Pentecost gave the initial thrust to their lives of evangelization.

They probably didn't realize it at first, but they had embarked on a journey of faith that would gradually transform their hearts, their attitudes, the basic drives of their lives. From the very beginnings of this journey—and this is important for us to remember—they constantly confronted themselves with the person, the words, and the love of the Lord. Following the Resurrection of Jesus, they had an ongoing experience of the Lord through prayer, the celebration of the Eucharist, and their mutual concern and affirmation.

On his part, Jesus compassionately accepted each of his followers wherever he or she was in the spiritual journey, allowing each the freedom to respond to the Lord in his or her fashion. He knew that their commitment was imperfect, dynamic, and subject to the laws of growth, and that each would grow in different ways and at different paces.

Jesus understood that growth would happen through listening and responding to God's daily revelations of himself through prayer and the Scriptures, through persons and events. He wants us to have the patience to realize that the renewal of our sense of values, the purification of our motives and desires, the total renewal of our vision of life is the work of a lifetime.

A MEMBER OF THE COMMUNITY OF FAITH

A study of Jesus' teaching on the kingdom of God shows that he intends us to mature spiritually and grow to our full personhood in a society of believers. This society is his church. And why is this? Because if we consider Christianity to be a series of good relationships with God, ourselves, and our neighbors, it follows that we are dependent on the love, support, and affirmation of others.

Only the rare few are called to seek the Lord in lonely isolation. Most of us need one another in order to proclaim and to live the Good News. Even the church—the society of the Lord— needs what sociologists call "support systems," so that its members may be loved, accepted, and affirmed and thus grow daily in their ability to love God and one another. In fact, it seems that we can only achieve our true uniqueness and our full stature in Christ in a community of faith and love, of concern and hope.

From every side today we receive reports of the growing alienation of various members of our society. At the heart of this alienation is the inability of many to handle the problem of daily stress, especially the demands of relating to others in a peaceful and mature manner. More than ever, the followers of Christ are being called to be healing ministers to society by the living witness they offer of affirming relationships in their own lives.

SHARED EXPERIENCES OF JESUS

What is the story of each apostle but a record of how he shared the message and the love that

Jesus had first given to him? They preached their memories of their personal experience of the Lord Jesus and they had an ever-present awareness of this growing relationship. And why should it be any different with us? The Lord may not grant to us the wonder-working gift of the apostles, but he never refuses that relationship with himself.

They gave their witness, as he had commanded them, by showing the impact of Jesus on each of their lives—by preaching the new "Way"—by sharing in his Passion and death when their time came. Like the church itself they realized that this mission was the natural consequence of their relationship with the Lord. This very relationship compelled them to go forth and preach the Good News. Even without the command of Christ they had an inner compulsion to share their memory of the Lord with anyone willing to listen to them. And so should we.

The Apostle Paul is a perfect example of this. Christ Jesus was the substance of his catechesis, the source of his power, the font of his wisdom, the very life he lived. He could truly say, "For me, to live, is Christ," because his daily life was a continual effort to identify himself with Christ, the power and wisdom of God. In this process, his life became remarkably integrated. And so, Paul wrote:

If our gospel can be called "veiled" in any sense, it is such only for those who are headed toward destruction. Their unbelieving minds have been blinded by the god of the present age so that they do not see the splendor of the gospel showing forth the glory of Christ, the image of God.

It is not ourselves we preach but Christ Jesus as Lord, and ourselves as your servants for Jesus' sake. For God, who said: "Let light shine out of darkness," has shone in our hearts that we in turn might make known the glory of God shining on the face of Christ.

(II Cor. 4:3-6)

The entire fourth chapter of the second letter to the Corinthians offers profound insights into Paul's view of his relationship to Christ Jesus and his presentation of it as a model of the relationship of every Christian to the Lord. Paul considered himself a servant of the Gospel for our sake and he was profoundly aware of how Jesus, the suffering servant, was reliving his life in Paul. His consciousness of this relationship gave a unique character to his own spirituality.

Questions to Ask Yourself

1. How would you evaluate your present relationship to our Blessed Lord?

2. What kind of personal commitment have you made to him?

3. Do you see a pattern of growth in your relationships to the Lord, your family, and others in your life?

4. Do you acknowledge to yourself the need of others to grow and mature in these relationships?

5. Are you convinced that God has given you a mission to share the gift of your faith?

6. When you pray or reflect on God, what is the habitual image you have of him?

Words to Remember

Eternal life is this: to know you, the only true God, and him whom you have sent, Jesus Christ. I have made your name known to those you gave me out of the world. As you have sent me into the world, so I have sent them into the world, I consecrate myself for their sakes now, that they may be consecrated in truth.

(John 17:3, 6, 18, 19)

CHAPTER V

Spirituality of the Disciples of Jesus

Most of us can probably relate rather well to the signs of a disciple of Christ given in the previous chapter. As members of a community of faith we have made a commitment to the Lord and we are more than willing to give witness to the Gospel by our words and our life. But we probably also believe that our commitment to Jesus would be greater if only we have seen him and listened to him "in the flesh." The first disciples would seem to have had a distinct advantage over us.

If this be our conviction, then we should select Paul the Apostle as our model of spirituality. Paul knew only the risen Christ, like ourselves, and his spirituality flowed from his relationship with the risen Lord. He insisted that we must look to Jesus, who inspires and perfects our faith.

No one had to remind Paul that the Christian vocation was a call to radical discipleship with the risen Jesus. The converted Saul was convinced that the truth, the power, and the love of God were enfleshed in the Incarnate Christ. Paul had unsuccessfully tried to convert the Athenians with human eloquence. Learning by this failure, he thereafter preached Christ as the power and wisdom of God. Later he could humbly write to the Corinthians:

As for myself, brothers, when I came to you I did not come proclaiming God's testimony with any particular eloquence or wisdom. No, I was determined that while I was with you I would speak of nothing but Jesus Christ and him crucified.

(I Cor. 2:1, 2)

In this matter we are not unlike Paul. Only slowly do we learn the lesson and internalize the truth that Jesus is the power, the wisdom, and the love of God. And only gradually do we truly understand the words of Paul: "For me to live is Christ." Like the first followers of Jesus, we slowly realize that we are called to relive the mysteries that the Lord first lived for us. With these truths in mind, we should strive to look more deeply into the heart of the Savior.

JESUS' INTIMATE RELATIONSHIP WITH THE FATHER

At the center of the heart of Jesus is a profoundly intimate and personal experience of Abba, his Father. Throughout his earthly career he submitted his humanity, his time, his talents in obedient love to his Father. He preached that eternal life was indeed this relationship to the Father and that he came to grant us an abundant share of this life. Throughout his last discourse (John, Chapters 14–17), Jesus gives precious insights into various aspects of his relationship with the Father, as in the following:

(Eternal life is this: to know you, the only true God, and him whom you have sent, Jesus Christ.) I pray also for those who will believe in me through their word [the disciples] that all may be one as you, Father, are in me, and I in you, that the world may believe that you sent me. I have given them the glory that you gave me, that they may be one, as we are one—I living in them, you living in me—that their unity may be complete. So shall the world know that you sent me, and that you loved them as you loved me. To them I have revealed your name, and

**I will continue to reveal it so that your love
for me may live in them, and I may live in
them.**

(John 17:3, 20–23, 26)

This gift of intimacy with God is obviously a
great gift; but we must remember that Jesus,
whose prayers to his Father are always heard,
prayed that he would live in us, that we would
share his oneness with the Father, and that the
Father's love would live in us.

These words and promises of Jesus should
refashion God's image for anyone who looks
upon him only as the Creator or Supreme
Lawgiver. Speaking to the Galatians, St. Paul
writes that we must have "the spirit of his Son"
to rightly pray the "Our Father": "The proof
that you are sons [or daughters] is the fact that
God has sent forth into our hearts the spirit of
his Son which cries out 'Abba' [Father]." (Gal.
4:6) The modern disciple should pray for this
gift of the Spirit.

THE SUPREME VALUE OF JESUS' LIFE

Because we seek the mind of Christ in all
things, we want his value system gradually to
replace our own. And the supreme value of

Jesus' life was the will of his Father. He was totally absorbed in the mission given him by the Father. His life was one of unconditional attachment to his Father's will. Perhaps this was the lesson of the Lord's temptations in the desert: no other love—nothing this life could possibly offer—could compete with that love. As we read in John, he would mirror the Father's will in all things:

> I solemnly assure you, the Son cannot do anything by himself—he can only do what he sees the Father doing. For whatever the Father does, the Son does likewise. For the Father loves the Son, and everything the Father does he shows him.
>
> (John 5:19, 20)

Jesus, the Son of Man, expressed his love for the Father by perfectly performing his will. He came to reveal his Father to us and to establish his renewed kingdom on earth. He taught us that this kind of love is the absolute value in life. It was the quintessential fact that gave all life, and death too, its ultimate meaning. Love—his love of the Father and of us—was not only as strong as death, it was stronger! This love was real, ever-present, unconditional, without ever counting the cost.

Growth in insight into the motivation underlying our varied activities is a gradual process. The Lord certainly has presented us with a sublime ideal, but complete dedication to the manifest will of God is a gift that normally comes by degrees. One thing is sure—once we make the great decision to refuse the Lord nothing he asks of us, our spiritual life seems to move into high gear. Our growing commitment to the will of God is surely fostered also by daily asking: Lord, what will you have me to do?

The Apostle Paul was overwhelmed by his consciousness of God's love for him. He kept repeating: "He loved me and delivered himself for me." This provided the inspiration, the support, and the strength for his life and apostolate. He needed no further inspiration. As an overflow of his ongoing relationship with the risen Christ, he also realized that he was able to love God and the brethren in the same way in which God loved him. Thus he writes to the Romans: "The love of God has been poured out in our hearts through the Holy Spirit who has been given to us." (Romans 5:5)

JESUS' LIFE OF LOVING SERVICE

If we were to attempt to summarize neatly the activities of our Lord, the Gospel statement would be most apt: "He went about doing good." He seems to have spent considerably more time healing the sick than he did teaching about the kingdom of God. His inner goodness constantly overflowed into his compassionate care and tender concern for all the spiritually, bodily, and temporally disadvantaged.

As usual, the first disciples were slow to see that these manifestations of the goodness of Jesus were signs that the kingdom of God was already among them. Instead of competing to follow this example, they fought over who should have the first places in the kingdom. Thus, we also hear the mother of the Zebedees (John and James) requesting places of greater honor for her sons.

We have no reason to make the same mistake. Today's disciple of Christ will express personal union with the Lord through loving and self-sacrificing service of the neighbor. As we serve Jesus in others, the likeness of the Lord within us grows. This compassionate service to others involves a certain "dying to self" and becomes a deeper sharing in the Passion of Jesus.

The Apostle Paul kept hammering away that our gifts are not for self-glorification and self-fulfillment, but for service, for community, for the building up of the body of Christ. (Eph. 4:15, 16) We must all build up the body of

Christ by using our gifts for the enrichment of all the members. Then, the body "will build itself up in love" and we will "grow to the full maturity of Christ the head." We might add that through our loving service to bring the mystical Christ to his "full stature," our own personal growth and our Christian maturity are advanced.

Questions to Ask Yourself

1. What is your habitual image of the heavenly Father? Does it resemble that of Jesus?

2. When you honestly confront your own system of values, how does the will of God rate?

3. How conscious are you of God's undying love for you?

4. How would you evaluate your loving service to others, starting with your own family?

5. Do you use your God-given gifts merely for your own self-satisfaction or in the service of those in need?

6. What, in your present thinking, do you believe your greatness consists of?

7. Does your present value system need refashioning? What do you intend to do about it?

Words to Remember

Anyone among you who aspires to greatness must serve the rest, and whoever wants to rank first among you must serve the needs of all. Such is the case with the Son of Man who has come, not to be served by others, but to serve, to give his own life as a ransom for the many.

(Matt. 20:26–28)

CHAPTER VI

Searching for a True Spirituality

According to a 1979 poll, America has over 80 million unchurched citizens. Among Catholics it is estimated that over 12 million are non-active in their communal religious practices. Half or more of these two groups expressed a desire for a deeper spirituality. This yearning for a deeper meaning to life is even more pronounced among the 130 million church-going Americans. All want a practical spirituality geared to life as it is today.

As we might expect, there are many descriptions of spirituality. Some see it as keeping the law of God; others as getting "close to God." Still others say it is trying to be a good person, while many look upon spirituality as one's relationship to his or her Lord. And there are many, especially among charismatic groups, who define spirituality as making Christ Jesus the Lord of one's life and the center and object of one's desires. All these descriptions, as we might expect, have certain elements of truth.

To become spiritual is indeed increasingly to experience Jesus Christ as the Lord of one's life and the object of one's religious strivings. A "spiritual" man or woman is simply one filled with the Spirit of the Lord. It is a Spirit that renews, heals, and refashions one in the likeness of the Lord and then overflows into all other relationships.

In essence our spiritual life is how we live the mystery of the life, death, and resurrection of Christ Jesus—what we call the Paschal Mystery of Jesus. This experience of the Lord does not lend itself to easy explanation. It is intensely personal, mysterious, deeply intimate, and subject to growth and decline. This process of making Jesus the Lord and center of your heart and life is the key experience of the Christian. It calls for a loving knowledge and an openness to his presence and action.

BEGINNING THE SEARCH

And how does one initiate the process of becoming a new person in the Lord? What can I do to deepen my personal relationship with Christ Jesus? A good start is the conviction that this project is more the Lord's work than one's own. Our efforts should be a response to the Spirit of God who is already at work within us. We become increasingly open and responsive to his comings, his power, his healing love.

Like the Apostle Paul, we must be willing to be "grasped by Christ" as we begin our efforts to live a "life on high in Christ Jesus" (Phil. 3:12, 14). A basic condition, I believe, is a sincere readiness to be changed by the Lord and a generous surrender of one's person, life, and talents to him. This disposition of spirit sets the stage for seeking a new identity in Christ and begins the blending of our two lives.

Given a basic willigness to let the Lord "take over," you start with your life just as it is. This is the stuff from which a deeper spirituality will be fashioned. Look over all your present relationships: with your God, your family, your friends, and all others who enter into your life-scheme. Gradually, let the Spirit of the Lord penetrate all these relationships. You will become changed for the better in the process.

In recent years, spiritual writers and directors have taught that initial training in the spiritual quest, and even in prayer, is training in personal relationships. They know that apart from these relationships, self-discovery and self-knowledge are not easily achieved. Even more important, they know that no growth as a person or as a Christian takes place outside of these relationships. Can someone be a real friend of God if he or she is incapable of human friendships? Can we achieve intimacy with the Lord if we are incapable of human intimacy? Can a person be truly spiritual if he or she is not a loving person?

A healthy, growing spiritual life demands interaction with others at all stages of the journey of faith. Our actions are a manifestation of who we are and an expression of our inner life. These actions will witness to the world how well we have internalized the message of the Gospel. And how do we detect the presence of the Lord within our hearts? It will be seen in:

the unending series of our daily decisions.

our faithfulness to personal prayer with Jesus.

our responsiveness to the valid needs of others.

our efforts to become a loving person.

our struggle to overcome our innate selfishness.

the manner in which we go about "doing good."

our patient endurance of the setbacks of life.

our practice of faith and trust, hope and love.

our reliance on the providence of God.

our consistent dedication to personal growth.

A NEW TYPE OF SPIRITUALITY?

Have we described a new kind of spirituality? While not spelled out in this fashion in a tract on spiritual theology, it certainly is authentic and practical. It is a spirituality that takes one where he or she is; is formed out of the stuff of one's daily life. As a matter of fact, it is the kind of spirituality we find in the life of our blessed Lord. Our efforts to become increasingly like the Master and to engage in the loving service of others will inevitably cause a dying of the unredeemed areas of self and the rising of a new and better self. And the process is unending. With each new effort and each new day, as our growth continues, the Lord becomes more real to us and his spirit becomes more mainfest in us. This process of dying and rising happens in all the relationships and interactions that constitute the fabric of our daily lives. And that is what we mean when we say spirituality is reliving the Paschal Mystery of Jesus!

To put your spirituality to the test, ask yourself questions such as these:

With what basic disposition do I start each day?

How do I approach my family, my Lord, my world?

In general, how do I interact with others?

How do I usually respond to the needs of others?

Do I simply perform religious practices or am I striving to become a new person in Christ?

What do I try to put into and get out of each day?

We will discover that our attempts to "put on" the Lord Jesus Christ lead to a delightful discovery—they deepen our experience of him. For example, to be compassionate toward the downtrodden of this world deepens our likeness to Christ, to whom we are witnessing in these acts of mercy and care. This ongoing inter-action is a key to spiritual growth. I become one with Jesus not merely by communicating with him in prayer, but by identifying with him in all my activities. The truth is that we are acting on these occasions as his "other self." It is the "one Christ loving himself," as St. Augustine expressed it.

EACH HAS A UNIQUE SPIRITUALITY

Perhaps a word of caution is necessary here. Each person's destiny and history is unique in relationship to the Lord. Each of us is a product of our age and heredity, of our education and cultural environment, to say nothing of our call to grace. The Lord calls us by a name given to no other and our personal experience of Christ will have distinctive qualities that are utterly our own. Some, like Mother Theresa, will discover and serve him among the diseased poor and dying; others, like Fulton Sheen, will serve him by preaching the Word of God; some align themselves with Christ in the quest for peace and social justice; while most lay down their lives in the humble and self-sacrificing struggle to raise a Christian family.

In one of his lectures, Father Karl Rahner, the Jesuit theologian, speaks of how our experiences of the Lord come to us through relationships with other persons:

No experience of God is possible, which is not mediated by an experience of the world. What mediates the experience of God is primarily man's relationships to other persons. This means that man's relationship to

other persons should be one of unconditional unbiased trust, of readiness to commit himself to his neighbor, to accept
responsibility for him—in other words, it
must become a relationship of love.

(*Doctrine & Life*, Apr/May, 1971)

Jorgen Moltmann, the Lutheran theologian,
offers another insight as to how to determine if
a church—or a spirituality—is authentically
Christian:

There is an inner criterion for every church
and theology that claim to be Christian, and
this criterion surpasses all political,
theological and psychological criticism
from outside:

IT IS THE CRUCIFIED HIMSELF.

When churches and theologies appeal to
him, they then appeal to their hardest judge
and their most radical liberator from lies,
from prestige and from anxiety. Churches
and theologies should be taken at their
word. AND THIS WORD IS THE WORD
OF THE CROSS! It is the criterion of their
truth and therefore the criticism of their un-
truth.

> The crisis of the church in today's society is not just the crisis of its adaptation or its risk to become a ghetto, but a crisis of its very existence as Church of the Crucified. Every just criticism from outside only points to its Christological crisis.
>
>   (*The Crucified God*, page 8)

These two great theologians are telling us, each in his own way, that there is no theology or spirituality apart from the person of Christ crucified. This spirituality is proven by loving relationships. And this implies a certain sharing in the Paschal Mystery.

Questions to Ask Yourself

1. How do you look upon spirituality? What is the special character of your own spirituality?

2. Do you look upon spirituality in terms of your relationships to God, self, others?

3. Does your spirituality affect every phase of your life?

4. Do you think that the Holy Spirit is drawing you to a special mystery of Christ or a special work within his kingdom?

5. Do you relate your setbacks and crosses in life to the death and Resurrection of Jesus?

6. Are you convinced that in your own unique way you are called to share in the complete life of our Lord?

7. Do you appreciate that this is the endeavor of a lifetime and that we are in a growing process?

Words to Remember

This treasure we possess in earthen vessels to make it clear that its surpassing power comes from God and not from us. We are afflicted in every way possible, but we are not crushed; full of doubts, we never despair. We are persecuted, but never abandoned. We are struck down, but never destroyed. Continually we carry about in our bodies the dying of Jesus, so that in our bodies the life of Jesus may be revealed. While we live we are constantly being delivered to death for Jesus' sake, so that the life of Jesus may be revealed in our mortal flesh.

(II Cor. 4:7–11)

CHAPTER VII

Communicating with Jesus

Prayer, like love itself, is not subject to easy definition. It has been called "conversation with God," "a lifting up of our minds and hearts to God," "an audience with the Divine Majesty," "an encounter with God," "an expression of our deepest being," "conscious contact with God," "loving attention to God," "a searching for reality," as well as many other descriptions.

I prefer to define prayer as "a personal communication with the Lord." This definition calls for a conscious involvement of the whole person in his or her attempts to contact the Lord. As a person is, so does he or she pray—the total person engages the Lord in prayer.

Earlier in this book, we have described the spiritual life as our unique response to God as he reveals himself in the present moment. God is forever breaking into our life through persons

and events, through his Word and the
sacraments, through joy and sorrow and, above
all, through the person of his beloved Son,
Jesus. This ongoing process will be especially
true in the dialogue we call prayer.

Recently, I ran across the following description of communication, which could also be
considered an apt description of prayer:

> **Communication is the ability of two per-
> sons to get through to each other. It implies
> a willingness to converse freely on all
> aspects of their shared lives. It is rooted in
> openness and responsiveness to each other.
> It calls for consistent effort to keep open
> the lines of communication. It is based on a
> deep reverence for each other's person.**

It is imperative that every true disciple of
Jesus remain in conscious contact with the
Master at each stage of life and mission. This
contact with the mind and heart of Jesus Christ
is impossible without frequent prayer.

Without prayer we will never achieve that
honest confrontation with self that marks the
beginnings of a wholehearted conversion to
God. Without prayer we will never develop a
sensitivity and responsiveness to the presence,

the revelation, and the action of the Lord. Without prayer we will not grow in conscious intimacy and deepened friendship with Jesus.

Prayer is the supreme activity of the human spirit. It is as essential to the spiritual life as breathing is to the body. Through this loving attention, we listen to God's Word and his will and reveal our own mind and heart to him. In the encounter that follows a gradual transformation of our spirit, motivations, life orientation takes place and we are, as St. Paul writes, "grasped by Christ."

All true prayer is transforming. However, it is not casual and occasional prayer that transforms us from within, but rather the habit of prayer. In prayer, the Holy Spirit gradually renews and refashions our understanding, memory, and heart with his healing power. At the beginning of our prayer life, he will empower us to engage in more frequent acts of faith, love, and trust. As these activities become more habitual, we become better disposed to receive the greater gifts of the Holy Spirit.

PRAYER—A CENTERING PROCESS

In recent years there has been an increasing amount of writing and reflection on what is

called the centering prayer. Simply put, centering prayer means to descend into one's deepest
self and to arrive at an experienced awareness
of God. Obviously all true prayer involves a
centering of spirit and mind, of memory and
heart on God as the supreme object of our seeking and our desires.

The term "centering prayer" was popularized
by the late Trappist writer, Thomas Merton.
His reflections were based on a spiritual classic
of the Middle Ages called *The Cloud of
Unknowing.* The Prayer of the Heart or The
Jesus Prayer are forms of a centering prayer.

Many persons today, like the ancient monks
in the desert, find this form of prayer to be
especially helpful. The following steps are
essential in this manner of communicating with
the Lord:

1. Select a quiet place where you can feel "at
   home" with the Lord. Assume a comfortable
   bodily position. Turn off your other preoccupations and close your eyes.

2. Try to let your body relax as much as possible. Let the habitual tensions flow out,
   breathing deeply to aid this process. Let
   your mind, body, and memory arrive at a
   gentle silence.

3. Center your total attention within, where the God of love and life dwells. Let a word or phrase arise in your consciousness—Jesus, Abba Father, Come Holy Spirit, or whatever expresses your present relationship to the Lord.

4. Repeat the word or words calmly and frequently, unless you feel called to complete silence. In a sense, this is your way of reaching out for and receiving the Lord. In the Jesus Prayer of *The Way of the Pilgrim*, another classic, the words were: "O Lord Jesus Christ, have mercy on me."

5. Conclude your prayer slowly, perhaps by deliberately reciting the Our Father or the Hail Mary. It is presumed in this prayer, as in all prayer, that if the Lord calls you to deeper silence or listening, you will accept the invitation.

OUR HABITUAL ORIENTATION TOWARD GOD

Success or failure in our prayer life depends greatly on our habitual orientation toward God. This means the frequency of turning to God or the centering of the powers of our soul upon him. To test our orientation we simply ask ourselves: How often do I turn to the Lord? How much time do I spend with him? How frequently do I find him in my thoughts? How much do I listen to him or converse with him? Am I inclined to "waste time" in his presence?

When someone is important to me I am disposed to give him or her top priority in my life. I am ready to give that person "prime time" in my day. Should it be any different with the Lord? If I am not convinced that he is the "pearl of great price," I will not be inclined to sacrifice the special times I give to other persons and events.

Prayer, then, is an expression of our habitual turnings to God. It measures accurately the degree of our desire for union with the Lord. Our orientation toward him grows and is intensified each time we center our mind, heart, and memory upon him. This does not happen, however, unless we spend time with him in frequent communication. We must begin to pray, and pray without ceasing. There is no other way to develop our friendship with the Lord.

We might add here that because prayer is an expression of our deepest desires, a divided heart will be quickly apparent in prayer. There is an intrinsic contradiction in asking the Lord to "take over" in our lives, while fixing our hearts on something not in tune with his will. This hardly means that our desires have to be in perfect accord with God before we start to pray, however, for it is precisely in the process of praying that our hearts are healed and restored to his likeness. As always, in our ongoing quest for the Lord, we start and restart wherever we are in the journey of faith.

PRAYER EXPRESSES OUR RELATIONSHIP WITH GOD

Your prayer tells a great deal about your present relationship with the Lord. Prayer is searching, seeking, begging, pleading, praising, worshiping, adoring, and thanking. But from one time to another, it is never quite the same because you are never the same. As with human communication, it is subject to growth and unfortunately to decline. It is yourself—as you are and as you determine to be. The whole person approaches God in prayer.

There is a key element of our prayer life whose importance is frequently overlooked, even though it affects greatly every aspect of our relationship to the Lord. That is the habitual image we have of our God. In short, what kind of God are you seeking in prayer? Or

how do you look upon the person with whom
you are trying to communicate?

Usually each of us has a certain image of the
Lord that comes to the fore when we enter into
conscious contact with him. A prayer that
centers on God as Creator will have a different
quality from one that turns to him as a personal
friend. One that honors God as supreme lawgiver will lack the spontaneity and trust of a
prayer that loves him as Abba, Father. A person
who habitually looks upon God as an all-seeing
judge will never have the joyful abandon of one
who seeks God as the infinite lover of humanity.

Each style of prayer is expressive of a different kind of intimacy. But whatever the style
of prayer, there will be no progress unless we
spend time with the Lord in this loving communication. His ongoing revelation to those
who seek him never stops. He eagerly anticipates each new audience with us. All we
have to do is to listen responsively and let him
take over as our guide, as St. Paul promises:
"The Spirit himself makes intercession for us
. . . for we do not know how to pray as we
ought." (Rom. 8:26).

Once we accept prayer as an ongoing
response to and communication with God as he
reveals himself from moment to moment, we
can readily see that there is no reason for a

dichotomy between work and prayer, between action and contemplation. Rather, the challenge for us is to be alert and responsive to the multiple ways he communicates with us. Prayer may be interwoven into any preoccupation and can be part of any relationship. The Lord may be met in the kitchen as well as in the chapel; he may speak to us in noise as well as in silence.

When we plan our special times with the Lord, however, it's wise to make a realistic appraisal of our day with its varied demands. When we study our days and our weeks, different patterns of involvements emerge. There are probably some quiet moments in many days, as well as periods of the week or year when we have more time to ourselves. If we truly value the Lord's friendship, we should make it a habit to put aside some prime time for him.

Finally, anyone seeking a conscious intimacy with the Lord should look to his or her heart. An essential predisposition for progress in prayer is a heart that is truly seeking the Lord and his love. As prayer intensifies our habitual orientation toward God, any turning from his known will is immediately reflected in our prayer life. This hardly means that God will abandon us to our sins and weaknesses. No matter what the state of our soul, when we reach out for him in trusting prayer, his healing love will remove the darkness from our minds and bolster the moral flabbiness of our wills.

He has promised to "make all things new," but only if we let him. And there is no better way than in the communication we call prayer!

Questions to Ask Yourself

1. What is your habitual orientation to the Lord?

2. When you pray, what is the usual image of God that comes through to you? Are you happy with this image?

3. How much prime time do you give to the Lord when you communicate with him in prayer?

4. Are you really convinced that God is the most worthwhile object of your thought and strivings?

5. Have you ever made the great decision—to try to refuse the Lord nothing he asks of you?

6. Do you listen to the Lord as attentively as you expect him to listen to you?

Words to Remember

So I say to you, "Ask and you shall receive; seek and you shall find; knock and it shall be opened to you. For whoever asks, receives; whoever seeks, finds; whoever knocks, is admitted. If you, with all your sins, know how to give your children good things, how much more will the heavenly Father give the Holy Spirit to those who ask him."

(Luke 11:9, 10, 13)

CHAPTER VIII

Some Modes of Communication

At the core of our personal relationship with the Lord is our inner life of conscious communication with him. The chief activity of this interior life is our response to the continuing revelation God makes of himself, his love, and his will.

RESPONDING TO GOD'S REVELATION

We will experience his presence and listen to his voice in several ways:

through *creation*. God has left his imprint on all of nature. All things were created through his Word. A spontaneous act of praise and wonder at the beauty of the mountains or the restless surgings of the sea can be a response to the myriad beauties of the Word.

through *people*. God speaks to us daily through our neighbor. People offer opportunities for relationships that deepen our likeness to the Lord or call for an increased sharing in the Paschal Mystery of Jesus. Our daily interactions with others present opportunities for personal growth and maturity.

through the *events of life*. As in the life of the Lord himself, these offer the stuff out of which our holiness will be fashioned. These events put us to the test, challenging our trust, our faith, and our faithfulness to the Father's will.

through *Jesus Christ*. He reminded us that when we look upon him we see the Father also. He is the manifestation of everything we will discover in the heart of Abba, our heavenly Father. And it is he who speaks when his words are heard in the church. As we read in Hebrews: "In the past God spoke to our ancestors many times and in many ways through the prophets, but in these last days he has spoken to us through his Son" (Heb. 1:1).

through *tradition*. Following Vatican II and more recent studies, we have an expanded view of tradition:

Tradition is now presented as embracing the whole life of the Church, its teachings, its worship and its practice. God is always speaking to everyone in the Church through the truths of revelation and the illumination of the Holy Spirit; and the Church is always responding with a faith that cannot fail.

(Decree on Divine Revelation.)

through the *Scriptures*. Sacred Scripture is the special revelation God has made of himself and his will to chosen men and women throughout human history. The Decree on Divine Revelation of Vatican II speaks inspiringly of this revelation:

Revelation is a vital communication of God to man. Through his living Word God enters into contact with those he addresses revealing himself and manifesting the secrets of his inward life and love. By this revelation then, the deepest truths about God and the salvation of man shine forth for our sake in Christ, who is both the Mediator and the fullness of all revelation.

In another place the decree states: "Only by faith and reflection on the Word of God can man come to recognize in every moment and at every place the God 'in whom we live, and move and have our being'" (Acts 17:28).

PRAYING WITH THE SCRIPTURES

The following are some practical hints on how to reflect prayerfully on sacred Scripture:

For a start, assume a comfortable bodily position and relax yourself by several moments of deep breathing. Gradually center your attention on the Lord.

Let your consciousness awaken to the presence of God. Try to be aware of his limitless love of you. Ask him to reveal himself to you and beg for the grace to be an attentive listener.

Select a passage of Scripture. It could be an event in the life of one of God's friends in the Old Testament, or a section from one of the Prophets, or an event, sermon, or miracle in the life of our Lord. Ask the Lord again to speak to you through his inspired text.

When something strikes you, respond peacefully to this inspiration. You may experience

God's love for you. You may sense forgiveness and healing. You may be given an insight never before possessed. Or you may become aware of a certain peacefulness in the Lord's presence.

These are just a few of the many ways that the Lord communicates with and speaks to you. Let them happen. Receive and relish them. Don't rush your response. The revelation of the Lord cannot be forced; it is possible to try too hard. Remember that God's revelation is a gift that comes from his goodness and not from the intensity of human efforts.

Do not be discouraged if you experience dryness or emptiness in your prayer. For his own wise reasons, God permits us to experience his absence as well as his presence. We have not been given the power to experience the Lord at will, but we do have the ability to pray without ceasing. The measure of our faith and progress in prayer is not the degree in which we are aware of the nearness of God. Sometimes it is helpful to talk to the Lord about one's emptiness and loneliness.

Perhaps we should mention here that the Lord speaks to us through the lights and insights given to others. This often happens in a charismatic prayer service or a bible study group. God will answer our prayer for understanding and insight, but he is quite unpredictable in the channels he chooses for his communication!

A SIMPLE FORM OF MEDITATION

There are times in our lives when we have a greater need for a framework of some kind to guide our reflections and aspirations in prayer. The fast pace of modern life has taken its toll and the everyday preoccupations of our minds and hearts make it difficult to center our spirit on the Lord's. While aware that each must approach God in his or her own way, we would like to suggest a simple method.

Preparing The preparation for prayer can be instantaneous. All it takes is an act of faith in the presence of the Lord. Then begin the work of centering your mind, heart, and memory on the Lord. This process is really an intensification of your usual orientation to God. This first turning to the Lord is very important; it shouldn't be half-hearted! It may often determine the success of your prayers, and should be based on the belief that our Lord eagerly anticipates this conversation with himself.

Reflecting The big question for many is: What shall I think about during prayer time?

The sacred Scriptures will supply a lifetime of material for your prayer reflections. Your special study should be, of course, the life, the mysteries, the words and deeds of Jesus Christ. Read a passage from the Bible and then reflect upon it. A spiritual reading book may be helpful, or some cassettes with meditations on the Christian life. In this area probably more helps are available today than ever before.

In fact, one of the simplest ways of praying is to discuss your day with the Lord. Review with him your goals and your failures, your problems and temptations, your joys and sorrows—all of your human involvements are material for prayer. This can be a deliberate and planned way of bringing Jesus into each facet of your daily life. At the very least, it will certainly provide an abundant source of material for your reflections!

Listening Our response to the unending revelation God makes of himself should be a lifelong process; but this is especially true in prayer. At each stage of our prayer, God will be involved with us. The dialogue of listening and responding, just as in human communication, should be continuous. He will speak to us at every stage of prayer, not only through his inspired Scriptures, but often in unexpected and unpredictable ways.

It follows that we must be careful to listen attentively to God in prayer. It is very easy to fall into the mistake of being too busy with our reflections and aspirations. We must give him the opportunity to get through to us.

Responding   Let me state again that Jesus will accompany us at each stage of the journey of prayer. Our sincere reflections on the life, words, and deeds of our Lord cannot remain sterile because his Spirit is leading us into ever deeper insights into the meaning of the mystery of Christ. He will inspire movements of praise and love, of petition and reparation that reach out for the Lord.

Let these actions flow in a simple, short, and unhurried manner. Don't be afraid to repeat them slowly. This is the heart of your communication with the Lord leading to a surrender of your life to him and causing a more intimate union with his heart.

Concluding   The conversation of prayer should conclude, as does any human communication, with heartfelt gratitude for the precious gifts the Lord has shared with you during prayer. Treasure in your memory the experiences and convictions that were the fruit of this prayer. Be aware of any new insight given to you. Did the Lord ask for a new or deeper commitment? After thanking the Lord for these gifts, we might ask him to continue the work of inner healing and grant us the courage and strength to follow through on his interior inspirations and directives.

Questions to Ask Yourself

1. Do you believe that the ultimate test of your prayer is your lifestyle?

2. In your life do you see renewed signs of the presence and action of the Holy Spirit: peace, joy, love, patience, kindness, compassion?

3. Do you look for the communication of the Lord, especially in his own revealed messages?

4. Does your prayer lead to a restoration of hope, a rekindling of faith, an increase of charity?

5. Does your prayer lead to renewed efforts to deepen your friendship and communion with Jesus?

6. Do you doubt the authenticity of your experiences of the Lord in prayer when you

see no change in your daily life? If you don't,
you should!

Words to Remember

For just as from the heavens
the rain and snow came down
And do not return there
till they have watered the earth,
making it fertile and fruitful,
Giving seed to him who sows
and bread to him who eats,
So shall my word be
that goes forth from my mouth;
It shall not return to me void,
but shall do my will,
achieving the end for which I sent it.

(Isaiah 55:10, 11)

CHAPTER IX

A Sign of Healing Love

There is one emotion of the human heart that few, if any, have not experienced at one time or another. For reasons right or wrong we have felt guilty. This experience of guilt may result from a genuine sin or failing, or it may be an emotion with little basis in reality.

Here we are concerned with actual sinfulness and what the Lord has done about it. Because he desires to remove all pain from our hearts and lives, we must search the Gospel to see what Jesus has done about our sins.

The first thing that we notice in his treatment of sinners is that he associated with them. In fact, he was publicly criticized for this. Never did he rebuke or condemn a sinner, or treat one harshly. The only persons he chastised were those who refused to admit their sins or who called their sins virtues. His actions always mirrored the forgiving mercy of his heavenly Father.

In his preaching he proclaimed the same message of forgiveness. Jesus said we must forgive seventy times seven; he told the story of the shepherd who left the ninety-nine to seek the sheep that was lost; and he reminded us, in the story of the prodigal son, that God celebrated the return of the errant son. He wanted us to know that in our Father's heart there is only forgiveness and mercy.

Because the Sacrament of Reconciliation (Penance) is a sign, we must ask what it is intended to symbolize. This sacrament is intended to be a celebration of God's healing love and a joyful proclamation of his forgiving mercy. For too long, too many of us have considered it merely a wonderful opportunity to unload our sins and be freed from our guilt!

A CELEBRATION OF GOD'S HEALING LOVE

The new rite of this sacrament is intended to highlight a truth that was perhaps understressed in the past: it attempts to make visible in a joyful and thankful way God's healing and forgiving action in our hearts and upon our persons.

We must stir up our faith to believe that in this sacrament we encounter the same Jesus that we read about in the pages of the Gospel. Through this sign, he warmly and lovingly invites each of us sinners to forgiveness, peace, and reconciliation. He heals and encourages, he teaches and consoles through the ministry of the church and the priesthood.

As he did at the beginning of his preaching campaign, he unequivocally demands a complete "change of heart"; but he has also promised to give us "a new heart" and a "new spirit" that guarantee the renewal and reform he seeks. Through this sacrament, he efficaciously speaks the word of forgiveness and pardon.

It is supremely important that we be convinced that we are approaching a merciful God passionately in love with us, else this sacrament will fall short in achieving the restored intimacy he longs to share with us. The overwhelming truth is that Jesus wants to heal us far in excess of our need for forgiveness and pardon. Jesus is "the Sign of Salvation" sent by the Father to speak words of forgiveness and to proclaim the words of absolution we long to hear.

We must add here that the church, the community of believers in Jesus, is also a sign of salvation on earth that gives witness to Jesus' healing and forgiving presence. Therefore, it must become a welcoming, forgiving, reconciling community that embraces every penitent sinner—how else could it pretend to be the authentic community of the Lord? The entire church must celebrate God's healing love and be a sign of reconciliation with God.

A SIGN OF RECONCILIATION WITH GOD

In recent times this sacrament has been called the Sacrament of Reconciliation. One reason for this title is that sin causes a certain alienation from ourselves, our neighbor, and our God. We become, as it were, a stranger in our own family and like the prodigal son need to be received back into the home and family of God. Reconciliation is necessary any time that our heart, mind, and actions are not in harmony with the will of God.

Our vocation is to be a loving member of the family of God. As affirming and supporting members of the community of Jesus we should assist one another in working toward our full development as unique human beings and children of God. When we fail through selfishness and sin, we need reconciliation, not only with God, but also with the offended members.

As Christians, we celebrate our reconciliation with God by being more perfectly reconciled with our fellow human beings. As peace-bearers, we are called to heal the wounds of division and alienation in families as in nations. We should struggle until every person has the right and the freedom to lead a life that is truly human, following the dictates of his or her own conscience.

In forgiving sin and reconciling the sinner to God, the church is the sign of the presence and the action of the merciful Savior. In the name of Jesus the church confronts sin—personal sin, structures of sin, or states of sin. By divine mandate the church strives to restore all persons to the health and wholeness of God.

The church's prayer in this Sacrament of Reconciliation is more than a fervent petition for pardon—it is a joyful, authoritative declaration that our sins are forgiven and we are reconciled to God. The fruits of the Paschal Mystery of Jesus, applied by the sacrament, remove all sins and heal their wounds.

THE STAGES OF FORGIVENESS

All the sacraments manifest the presence of Jesus in some manner and continue his saving action in our hearts. His Incarnation strikingly proclaims that healing love is at the very heart of redemption.

The new rite of penance tries to teach us that we must be concerned not only with individual sinful actions, but also with the core of selfishness and sinfulness from which these activities proceed. Complete conversion demands more than an external refashioning of our moral manners. It calls for a thorough renewal and healing from within. Anger and sloth, jealousy and envy, sensuality and neglect of God's worship spring from a heart that is not at peace with itself or with God.

Because this sacrament is intended to be an encounter in faith, love, and trust with the healing Christ, it takes into account the evil tendencies within us. Through it we approach the Savior as did the people of the Gospel —with sincere sorrow for our misdeeds and with complete trust in his willingness to grant forgiveness. Only then is the sinner ready to present himself or herself for absolution and pardon.

The following are some of the dispositions needed before we, as sinners, present ourselves to Jesus the Savior for forgiveness:

First, we must stir up our faith in what this sacrament is all about. We acknowledge the presence and power of the healing Jesus acting through this sacrament.

After a nonworrisome but objective examination of our spiritual state, we humbly confess our sinfulness.

We believe and trust that he can and will heal and forgive us. Our Lord always found this disposition of soul irresistible.

We humbly ask for forgiveness remembering that this sacrament glorifies the mercy of God and restores our innocence.

We accept God's forgiveness. This may seem obvious, but there are some who doubt the forgiveness of God because they fail to forgive themselves.

We "go in peace." God has accepted us as we are, he has forgiven us far beyond our expectations, and he has lovingly healed us. Peace, as promised, is his gift to us! And we try to sin no more.

Words to Remember

I will give you a new heart, and place a new spirit within you, taking from your bodies your stony hearts and giving you natural hearts. <u>I will put my spirit within you and make you live by my statutes, careful to observe my decrees. I will sprinkle clean water upon you to cleanse you from all your impurities, and from all your idols I will cleanse you. You shall be my people and I will be your God.</u>

(Ezekiel 36:26, 27, 25, 28)

A POSITIVE EXAMINATION OF CONSCIENCE

The response to these questions could be:

"Lord, have mercy!"

For the times I have taken you for granted . . .

For failing to study and reflect on my God-given faith . . .

For not seeing and serving God in my family members . . .

For lack of concern or interest in others . . .

For having revealed truths that hurt others . . .

For the times I refused to help others in need . . .

For any bad example I have given to others . . .

For the times when I was a divisive rather than peace-making influence on others . . .

For the times I returned anger for anger . . .

For judging the inner motivations of others . . .

For discriminating against those of different race or religion . . .

For being more demanding of others than of myself . . .

For going along with the crowd when I shouldn't have . . .

For not practicing what I preach to others . . .

For the chief sin I commit in my life . . .

For failing to forgive others their faults against me . . .

For failing to take the first steps of reconciliation . . .

For being jealous or envious of others . . .

For failing to keep my promises to God and others . . .

For any deceit or dishonesty in my life . . .

For not being sufficiently aware of God's eternal love . . .

For not praying to God in times of crisis . . .

For those I have hurt or injured through my anger . . .

For not listening to my family when they need me . . .

For all my past sins of sensuality and unchastity . . .

For my lack of trust in God's providential care of me . . .

For not being the person God wants me to become . . .

For failing to accept and forgive myself . . .

For not turning instinctively to God in times of need . . .

For not being more responsive to the Holy Spirit . . .

For any other failings that I might have overlooked . . .

For anything in my life that is displeasing to God . . .

For not making Jesus my Way, my Truth, and my Life . . .

Lord, have mercy!

CHAPTER X

The Sign of His Presence

In the pages of this book we have been speaking of spirituality in terms of our relationship with the Lord, and through him, with the other members of his community of faith, the church. Like other human relationships, our relationship with Christ involves times of presence and times of absence. Jesus entered into intimacy with us not only by coming to earth, but also by leaving it. During his farewell supper, Jesus tried to teach this lesson to his apostles:

> Yet I tell you the sober truth: It is much better for you that I go. If I fail to go, the Paraclete will never come to you, whereas if I go, I will send him to you.
>
> (John 16:7)

Jesus knew that for all time the heart of the church would be the presence of himself and his Spirit in the hearts and lives of his followers. Before he left he would give them a "living memorial" that would guarantee that presence. Through his physical departure from earth, he became our very food and drink—the life of our souls. The disciples received the fullness of the Spirit only after Jesus had ascended into heaven. Before he left he gave them a unique and beautiful memory—one that made possible an even greater intimacy with him.

In all the history of friendship and love there has never been a memorial like this—a living memorial that continues his incarnational presence, bringing with it his power, his love, and his companionship. As faithful followers and loving friends, we should treasure and store up in our memory the words and deeds of Jesus. But like the disciples, we must do more: we must remember him in that special way he commanded when he said: "Do this in remembrance of me."

The basic effort in the Eucharistic celebration will always be to remember Jesus Christ. The apostles met every Sunday to celebrate the Eucharist and so to recall his death and Resurrection. We come together as a community of faith called and saved by Christ to remember his act of healing love. Jesus, the host, invites us to assemble in the name of his Father for this act of thanksgiving and praise.

The presence of Jesus is most significant. It is more than just the memory of what Jesus did; rather, Jesus is doing it again—with us—in a symbol that contains the reality it expresses. He is the gift offered to the Father. He is the food that is received. He is the priest who offers the sacrifice. Jesus' presence permeates the whole of this reality. He is memorialized in himself and in each of his mysteries. To remember is to re-present.

PROCLAIMING THE MYSTERY OF CHRIST

In the Liturgy Constitution of Vatican II we find this statement: "The Eucharist is the outstanding means whereby the faithful express in their lives and to others the mystery of Christ and the real nature of the Church." In other words, it is the outstanding way to remember Jesus Christ.

And why is this so? Because in this Paschal Mystery—the Passion, death, and Resurrection of Jesus—he perfectly fulfilled his Father's designs and reconciled us to the Father. This crowning work in the life of the Savior was the wholehearted expression of the total self-surrender, the fullness of worship, and loving obedience present in the heart of Jesus, the priest and victim.

It may be said that on Calvary our blessed Lord summed up his entire earthly life in one supreme act of self-sacrificing love. On the first Good Friday he offered to his Father everything he ever wanted or demanded from humankind. Now the Father expects us to offer ourselves in union with his Son so that there may be, as Augustine wrote, "One Christ offering himself." The Father has predestined in Christ. . .he wishes us to be in conscious contact with him at each stage of the journey of faith, but especially in the celebration of the Eucharist.

If the Father had given us only a beautiful memory of the life and death of Jesus it would be indeed an overwhelming gift. But his love compelled him to do much more—he granted us the opportunity to become personally involved in the renewal and re-presentation of this mystery. Through the Eucharist, containing all the realities of the mystery of Jesus, we offer him the living heart of Jesus, his well-beloved. Through this "living memorial" the Father receives perfect worship and we receive the fruits of the death and Resurrection of Jesus.

With these reflections in mind, it is very difficult to understand nonactive Catholics who bypass the Eucharist. They usually say: "I go direct to God. I pray in my own way. I just don't feel the need for the institutional church." What they are doing is good, but not good enough! What about remembering the Lord in the special way he commanded? Isn't it rather presumptuous to select one's own way of worshiping when the Lord has given us a most perfect way of uniting our worship with his?

The Constitution on the Liturgy states: "From the Liturgy, and especially from the Eucharist as a font, grace is poured forth on us and the sanctification of all men in Christ and the glorification of God, to which all other activities of the Church are directed as to their end, is achieved in a most efficacious way." No wonder then that we are called to a conscious, intelligent, and active participation in the liturgy, which represents the mystery of Jesus. This is a precious gift of the Lord; and we would be foolish to disregard it in favor of our own approach to God.

THE HEART OF THE MATTER

One of the most loving and most lovable of popes, John XXIII was famed the world over for being so open, so approachable, so thoroughly human. He seemed to have a special charism for integrating the human and the divine in his spirituality. To appreciate the depth of his spirituality one must read his autobiography, *The Journal of a Soul*. In this work he writes of how he blended his love for the heart of Christ with that of the Blessed Sacrament:

Every time I heard anyone speak of the Sacred Heart of Jesus or of the Blessed Sacrament, I feel an indescribable joy. . . . These are loving appeals from Jesus who wants me wholeheartedly there, at the source of all goodness, his Sacred Heart, throbbing mysteriously behind the Eucharistic veils. The devotion to the Sacred Heart has grown with me all my life.

It is to the heart of Jesus that I must look for a solution in all my troubles. I want the devotion to his Heart, concealed within the Sacrament of love, to be the measure of all my spiritual progress. I am determined to give myself no peace until I can truly say I am absorbed into the Heart of Jesus.

Pope John has shown us the inner disposition needed to participate perfectly in the offering of the Eucharist—it is to be united as much as possible with the disposition of the heart of Christ. The more our dispositions are attuned to his heart, the more our gift will please the Father.

The heart of the Savior is the same yesterday, today, and tomorrow. The healing love and compassionate care of Jesus are present and active at every Mass drawing all humanity to himself. Of all the realities on this earth, this is the one in which the Father finds his greatest delight—and in ourselves when we are united to that heart.

THE POWER OF THE PASSION

Throughout this book we have spoken of the need to internalize the Gospel message, to seek a wholehearted renewal of heart and soul, to "put on" the Lord Jesus in all things. One of the greatest means of achieving these goals is our presence at and our celebration of the Eucharist. As St. Thomas Aquinas wrote, the Eucharist contains Christ and the whole power of his Passion and it is from the opened heart of Jesus on the cross that these blessings flow.

Just as he first sent Jesus to this earth, the eternal Father with each Eucharistic communion sends his Son on a special mission to your soul. There the Father and the Holy Spirit mutually breathe forth the peace and love, the power and strength of God. Jesus the Lord comes in unreserved self-surrender. As divine healer he comes to heal you of the wounds of your sins and selfishness. As faithful friend he comes to place his strength, power, and wisdom at your disposal. As perfect lover, wishing to be your other self, he comes to be your way, your truth, your very life!

The special grace of Eucharistic communion is also the goal of our Christian lives—union with the heart of Jesus in love. The special effect of this Bread of Heaven is to unite us to and gradually transform us into Christ. However, this transformation is an ongoing process. God's revelation of himself is a gradual one and our relationship with him is a growing one. Therefore, we must activate our faith to make us more responsive to this encounter with Jesus. Our trust should prompt us again to place our life in his hands. And our humble love should petition his Spirit to take over in our lives and be the dynamic force behind all our activities.

Questions to Ask Yourself

1. Is the Eucharist the outstanding way by which you remember Jesus Christ and what he has done for you?

2. Do you look upon this sacrament as an indispensable source of the Spirit of Jesus?

3. At Mass do you try to unite yourself with the dispositions of the heart of Christ in this sacrifice?

4. Do you believe that the Mass is a God-given way for the children of God to worship perfectly their Father in heaven?

5. What is ordinarily the state of your attention when attending Mass?

6. What effect does your celebration of this memorial of the Lord have upon your daily life?

Words to Remember

Let me solemnly assure you, if you do not eat the flesh of the Son of Man and drink his blood, you have no life in you. He who feeds on my flesh and drinks my blood has life eternal, and I will raise him up on the last day. For my flesh is real food and my blood real drink. The man who feeds on my flesh and drinks my blood remains in me, and I in him. This is the bread that has come down from heaven. Unlike your ancestors who ate and died nonetheless, the man who feeds on this bread shall live forever.

(John 6:53–56, 58)

CHAPTER XI

The Compassionating of Jesus

In the Christian vocabulary, love is a word deserving of special reverence because as St. John wrote: "God is love, and he who abides in love, abides in God and God in him." Despite this statement of the Apostle of Love, probably no other word has been more trivialized in song, speech, and story. Perhaps the only fair way to treat love is to define it by deeds and not by words.

Charity is, therefore, the sign above all others that stamps us with the seal of a disciple of Christ. If Jesus is indeed the vine and we are the branches, his healing, affirming, forgiving love will be the significant quality in our lives. We are blessed in the fact that there is no doubt about the special commandment of the Lord: "This is my commandment: love one another as I have loved you (John 15:12), and he also tells us "to live on in my love" (John 15:9).

In the early days of his pontificate, Pope John Paul II explained how our love should embrace all the needy and he gave the reason why:

> Charity is not just the fruit of sentimental or fleeting compassion . . . IT IS DEEPEST LOVE BROUGHT TO EACH AND EVERY MAN ESPECIALLY THOSE IN NEED. Its justification and its dynamism have their root in the value of man and his right to a decent life. It is enough to know that he is in need. . .of food, shelter, clothing, a job, consolation in his solitude, a visit, support for himself and his family. And if this human person is so valuable in our eyes, it is because he is valued so highly by God first. IT IS BECAUSE CHRIST IDENTIFIED WITH HIM. It is because Christ wishes us to treat others as we would like them to treat us. . . .

In the early days of his conversion, Malcolm Muggeridge, the English writer, inquired as to where he could find someone who exemplified in his or her lifestyle Christ's command of love. He was directed to the slums of Calcutta in India, where he met Mother Theresa and studied her work among the diseased and dying. Profoundly impressed by her holiness and her ministry to the dying, he returned home and wrote a book, *Something Beautiful for God.*

This modern Veronica, who has spent almost thirty-four years compassionating the suffering Christ through his sick and dying members, spoke of what she called the "greatest evil":

The biggest disease today is not leprosy or tuberculosis but rather the feeling of being unwanted, uncared for and deserted by everybody.

The greatest evil is lack of love, the terrible indifference towards one's neighbor who lives at the roadside assaulted by exploitation, poverty and disease.

The unwanted are hungry not for food but for love. They are thirsty not for water but for peace. They are homeless not for shelter but for understanding. Even your feeble efforts will bring much fruit, if you bring God into your life. If you can love and share, you will be happy, genuinely so.

Have you been selfish so far—and who is not? Be converted. Be kind and merciful. Be the living expression of kindness—kindness in your face—kindness in your eyes —kindness in your warm greeting.

LET NO ONE EVER COME TO YOU WITHOUT GOING AWAY BETTER AND HAPPIER!

When the Nobel Peace Committee conferred its annual prize for peace on Mother Theresa, it echoed the words of Pope John Paul: "A feature of her work has been respect for the individual human being, for his or her dignity and innate value. The lowliest, the most wretched and the dying have at her hands received compassion without condescension based on the reverence for man."

THE OUTREACH OF LOVE

Few are called to nurse the diseased and dying poor in a Calcutta slum; but none of us is exempt from the imperative of charity to seek out and serve Jesus among the suffering needy. There are as many ways of doing this as there are human needs. Helping to provide food, shelter, clothing, a job are some of the more obvious ways. But what about visiting or praying with the sick, a phone call or a letter to someone agonizing in loneliness, patience with a neurotic friend or relative, encouraging a friend in his faith struggles?

Isn't it true that we tend to fail in the less obvious ways of compassionating Jesus through his suffering members—like overlooking the faults of those we know, or affirming someone we know when he or she seems least deserving of love or attention, or listening deeply not only to the words, but also the heart of a member of our family, or being nonjudgmental when a relative or friend unburdens his or her heart? Doesn't Jesus reveal himself to us through all these avenues of need?

The practice of this kind of compassion is a deeper sharing in the Passion of Jesus. And its rewards are impressive. Your healing compassion removes some of the ugliness of body or spirit from those scarred by life. It makes the presence and love of Jesus real to them. And this kind ministry to your suffering neighbor conforms your heart to Christ's!

CONFRONTING THE UNLOVABLE

A common problem for most of us is how to deal with the unlovable people who touch our lives. To find our answer we must search the pages of the Gospel and study how Jesus responded to the various needs of all who approached him.

He spent an amazing amount of time with the unwanted and the unloved. The lame, the leper, the lunatic, the beggars, the adulterers, the unspiritual, the unhappy seemed to get preferential treatment from him. Jesus never seemed to be turned off by the thoughtlessness of those constantly pressing in upon him. He always forgave, sometimes healed, and never judged.

His compassion compelled him to respond to their suffering with care and concern. His gracious mercy reached out for the sick and sorrowful, the weak and the sinner, the fearful and the discouraged. He wanted to remove from their lives anything that hurt them. The apostles looked upon Jesus as a most compassionate man.

This tells us something. We should never be shocked when we find our neighbor lacking in beautiful human or divine qualities. We are here to continue the compassionate work of Jesus. Our loving service will help to restore their human dignity, to heal their bodily and spiritual wounds, to restore to them the consciousness of their self-worth. This, more than any preaching, will lead them to God.

This kind of healing love is the vocation of every Christian. Each of us has been invited to offer our humanity—our life, energies, and talents—to the Lord that he may continue to go about doing good. That's why St. Paul sums up the imperative of the whole Gospel in a single sentence: "The whole law has found its fulfillment in this one saying: 'You shall love your neighbor as yourself'" (Gal. 5:14).

OUR NEED FOR AFFIRMATION

Our blessed Lord, John Paul II, and Mother Theresa all teach us a profound lesson that flows from the inmost heart of the Gospel: reverence and love for the unwanted and the unloved leads to their conversion and transformation into renewed and recreated human beings.

This means that the only way to free a person from feelings of self-alienation and self-rejection is to befriend and love him and thus build up his feelings of self-worth. Normally, we grow as human beings or as Christians only in an environment of acceptance and support, of friendship and of love.

This affirmation is solidly based on the absolute dignity and worth of each person in the sight of God, regardless of his or her present situation. It demands acceptance and love of that person as a child of God no matter how badly he or she may have abused the gift of life. We have an awesome responsibility to affirm the worthwhileness of every person who touches our life.

Would you like to share the power of God and have the ability to be a healing influence on everyone who approaches you? Then practice the Godlike affirmation of accepting, loving, being concerned about each person whom you encounter.

Remember that only when a person is aware of being loved does he or she have a sense of self-worth and security. Only then can he or she be freed from childish attention-getting maneuvers, vain boasting, and fears of not being liked. St. John wrote beautifully, "We love because he has first loved us," and we are empowered to love—to fulfill the essential of the Gospel—only because we are convinced that we have been found worthy of love. Only when we have this consciousness will we take the risk of loving others.

THE LEAST OF THE BRETHREN

Some of the directives of our blessed Lord are so all-embracing that a single saying could provide the motivation for an entire lifetime.

Such a saying is: "As often as you did it for one of my least brothers, you did it for me" (Matt. 25:40).

I don't think we have too much difficulty in placing the neglected poor, the diseased and dying, the refugees of war, and the rejects of society in that category of "the least." But has it ever occurred to you that you yourself may be "the least of the brethren?" At least in your own mind.

In my experience, all too many religious people are not very fair in judging their self-worth and are much too harsh in judging their moral worth. This is the unfortunate result of a religious background that overstressed their failures in life and understressed their constant efforts to be good persons. Becoming rather repressive toward themselves, they perhaps inhibited their basic goodness from growing and maturing normally.

Remember that Jesus told us to love our neighbor as ourselves. This means not only that our treatment of ourselves is the measure and norm of our love for others, but also that we should exercise the same gracious love and kindly forgiveness toward ourselves that we do to others. Once we achieve this humble and sincere self-love we will be able to love our fellow man more easily. This well may be an area of our spiritual life that calls for more attention.

Begin by believing that you are a unique and beautiful creation of God. He has given you a name offered to no other. Be kind, gracious, and forgiving of yourself. Love and accept yourself just as you are in the journey of life, because that is exactly what God does!

Questions to Ask Yourself

1. Do you try to discover the suffering Jesus in those in physical, mental, or spiritual need?

2. Are you sufficiently attentive to the needy in your own household? Do you truly listen to them?

3. What is your present level of concern for the needy of this world?

4. If God has given you more than others, to what extent do you share in his gifts?

5. Are you inclined to judge the "have-nots" in this life, or do you help others simply because they are in need?

6. To what extent do you use your talents in the quest for peace and justice among the underprivileged?

Words to Remember

For I was hungry and you gave me food, I was thirsty and you gave me drink. I was a stranger and you welcomed me, naked and you clothed me. I was ill and you comforted me, in prison and you came to visit me . . . . I assure you, as often as you did it for one of my least brothers, you did it for me.

(Matt. 25:35, 36, 40)

CHAPTER XII

Christ in You—
Your Hope of Glory

Frequently, as I walk the bustling streets of a crowded city watching the shoppers and passersby, I ask myself: What are their dreams made of? What do they want from their lives? What motivates their daily activities? Are they reaching out for the "unreachable star" or the "impossible dream"?

Isn't it true that their driving force is hope, whether that hope be for a diamond ring, a better salary, or a new car or home? Ernest Block, who spent forty years studying it, wrote that hope is the principal human motivation. He added that nothing is ever achieved without hope. It was present at the start of every great human achievement and its absence signaled the death of other human endeavors. Hope is the stuff that dreams are made of. Without hope, survival on this planet is impossible.

Many recent books deal with the various neuroses that afflict us today. Victor Frankl claims to have discerned a universal neurosis in modern culture. He calls it "the loss of a will to meaning." This is but another way of saying that our contemporaries lack a value system that makes life truly meaningful. To put it bluntly: they are losing hope and confidence in themselves and in life.

For the Christian, hope is a precious gift of God that makes possible wholehearted trust in the providence of a wise, powerful, and loving God. This trust is securely based on God's unfailing faithfulness to all his promises to us.

In these pages the Christian life has been presented as a deep personal relationship with the Lord Jesus. The act of abiding in Christ, which is the special fruit of this relationship, constitutes our claim to eternal life and gives deep meaning to this present life. As St. Paul writes: "Christ in you [is] your hope of glory."

THE MAKE UP OF HOPE

An understanding of the dynamics of hope is helpful because the personal history of salvation of every one of us seems to include a profound testing of hope. Hope deals with the covenant God has made with his people and his faithfulness in keeping the promises that are the substance of that covenant. While his faithfulness stands out in the New as well as the Old Testament, he never hesitates to put the people of God to the test.

When we study the Bible, we usually discover four stages in the covenant God makes with his people:

1. He makes a promise to a person or group.

2. Later, he fulfills that given promise.

3. He then apparently takes it away.

4. Finally, he restores it more perfectly.

A television series called "Great Stories of the Bible" included an excellent presentation of Abraham, the father of the chosen race. First, when Abraham was an old man, God promised him that he would be the father of many nations. Not too long afterward, God blessed Abraham's previously sterile wife, Sarah, with a son. This son, Isaac, became the only hope for the fulfillment of God's promise. God then seems to undermine his own promise by asking Abraham to slay his son as a sacrifice to God. When Abraham obediently prepares to do so, God intervenes and Isaac is saved. Isaac, of course, later begets Jacob who becomes the father of the twelve tribes of Israel.

Or consider the story of the Virgin Mary. God sends the Angel Gabriel to announce to her that she has been chosen to mother the Incarnate Son of God, Jesus Christ. She believes in the power of God, conceives her son, and later gives birth to him on that first Christmas. Jesus becomes a man, preaches the kingdom of his Father, is persecuted and put to death. It seems, once again, that God has failed in his promise. But Jesus conquers sin and death, founds his church, and is always with us.

HOPE—THE ROOT OF RENEWAL

Hope is the basic element of renewal and the church cannot hope to become the renewed bride of Christ without it. We can't help wondering if the alarming increase in numbers of nonactive Catholics, as well as the large numbers who have left the priesthood and the religious life, might not be traced at least in part to a lack of hope—or a lack of Christian meanings. Discouragement, which is lack of hope, might be called an attempt to escape one's personal encounter with the Passion of Christ. It is forgetting that all growth—human or Christian

—involves some pain and discipline.

True hope, on the contrary, based on the limitless power and mercy of God, should never run short. We become discouraged only when we rely too much on our own talents and powers, forgetting the reassuring words of Christ: "With me you can do all things and without me you can do nothing."

The crisis of faith so evident today also means that hope is in crisis because faith provides the substance of hope. We are already subjected to "future shock" arising from the ever-accelerating tempo of change in our culture, and even in some of our religious practices. In the realm of religious belief and practice, the faithful don't take too easily to change. There is a great emotional attachment here—unfortunately even in accidentals.

When we consider some of the current debates in the church today, we wonder if Jesus sometimes gets lost in the shuffle. The questions of legitimate dissent in the church—the problems of divorce and remarriage, the question of women's rights, and many others—all call for reasonable and charitable debate; but they are not the fundamental questions of Christianity. We simply cannot let these problems distract us from the person of Jesus Christ and the promises of God.

SHARING THE PASSION OF JESUS

I am convinced, after reading the signs of the times, that the Church of Christ has been undergoing a profound purification in the years following the closing of Vatican II. Her hope in the promises of God has been tested in a way not unlike that of Abraham and the Virgin Mary. Some authors, with an approach similar to St. John of the Cross in his *The Dark Night,* have called this purification a dark night of the sense and of the human spirit.

Putting aside theological terminology, they are simply saying that the sensual and spiritual part of us needs a healing purification before we can be completely renewed in Christ. This should not surprise anyone sincerely striving for a renewed life in Christ. We all experience the need for this kind of healing and we realize that it demands deeper levels of hope and faith. These spiritual crises are really an invitation for a more profound sharing in the Passion of Jesus, so that we may be prepared for a deeper manifestation of the risen Christ within us. Unfortunately, it seems that all too many of us did not recognize this period as a crisis of growth, and not heeding the Spirit of the Lord, dropped out of the spiritual struggle.

I am sure that if you said to the confused, average Christian of today: "Do you know that you're being tested by God, just as were Abraham and Mary?" your sanity would be questioned. But we are undergoing the same trial of hope. The solid church of our youth seems to be floundering; discipline seems to be lost; doctrine is questioned; the Scriptures seem to be assaulted from all sides; the authority of the Vicar of Christ, the Pope, is ignored.

Yet our hope tells us that Christ would never abandon the church he promised to be with until the end of time. God is still absolutely faithful to his promises. Our securities are challenged, but God is infinitely unchanging in his love and providential care of us. We must study prayerfully these signs of our times and say: Lord, what are you trying to tell me—and what would you have me do?

SOME CONCLUSIONS REGARDING HOPE

You have only one lifetime to practice hope. Circumscribed by birth and death, it is given only in space and time. It always reaches out for fulfillment and is never possessed perfectly in time. It takes time to grow . . . as a Christian . . . as a lover . . . as a disciple of Christ. Sheer physical, mathematical time. So many minutes, hours, and days. Time and attention too—careful, concerned, consistent attention.

But we must remember that from the beginnings of his revelation to its ultimate conclusion, one great truth stands out: God is absolutely faithful to all his promises. His ongoing revelation of himself and his will through the Scriptures, his Church, persons, events, and the world continues to this very moment. His wise and loving Providence embraces the least of our actions and preoccupations. His unbelievable mercy, the outstanding characteristic of his Providence, always embraces us.

Jesus Christ is truly risen and lives within us. He is our light, our direction, our friend, our Savior, our joy, our very life. The Christian life is the life of Jesus within us, possessed by grace, and become alive by hope, faith and charity. There is not a moment of our lives when he does not present himself to us in the guise of some person, event or thing. In the depths of our spirit, he and the Father breathe forth the Spirit, who is the source of our Christlikeness in our thoughts, desires and deeds.

Saint Paul writes that we are "awaiting the revelation of the sons of God." But as we await the full revelation, we study the signs of our times, to discern the presence or the action of the Lord in current happenings. In our personal history of salvation, we must listen to God and follow him at this very moment. We have to look at Christ within us, "our hope of glory," and firmly believe with St. Paul:

"With him has God not given us all good things!"

Questions to Ask Yourself

1. Are you really convinced that "to those who love God all things work unto good"?

2. Are you as faithful to prayer and your daily communication with the Lord when he seems far away as when you feel his presence?

3. Do you base your hope for eternal life on your own efforts or on the mercy of God?

4. Try to reflect on the ways that you can practice the virtue of hope today and see how you can grow in this theological virtue.

5. When you are in crisis, spiritual or otherwise, do you say: "Lord, what are you trying to tell me?"

6. In times of need, do you seek for encouragement from the promises of Christ, the Unchanging Lover?

Words to Remember

Everything written before our time was written for our instruction, that we might derive hope from the lessons of patience and the words of encouragement in the Scriptures. May God, the source of all patience and encouragement, enable you to live in perfect harmony with one another according to the spirit of Christ Jesus, so that with one heart and voice you may glorify God, the Father of our Lord Jesus Christ.

(Romans 15:4–6)

CHAPTER XIII

The Call to Evangelization

Following the close of the Second Vatican Council in 1965 there have been increasing signs of the advent of a second Pentecost in the Church of Christ.

One of the more striking signs of the activity of the Holy Spirit following Pentecost was the generous and fervent fulfillment of Jesus' final command: "Go into the whole world and proclaim the Good News to all creation" (Mark 16:15).

Therefore, we would seriously doubt that another Pentecost is really taking place unless we witness a renewed and enthusiastic proclamation of the Good News of Salvation. The signs of this proclamation can be found in the following events:

the 1974 Synod of Bishops in Rome on the theme and necessity of evangelization.

the apostolic exhortation ("Evangelii Nuntiandi") on evangelization of Pope Paul VI in 1975.

the programs of evangelization now taking place in most American Catholic dioceses.

the dedicated willingness of increasing numbers of American Catholics to share in this primary work of the church, following the deepened consciousness that all share the mission of bringing the Good News to all humanity.

This chapter will attempt to summarize the key truths of the apostolic exhortation of our late Holy Father, Pope Paul VI: *The Gospel Must Be Proclaimed.*

JESUS IS THE FIRST EVANGELIZER

Our Lord Jesus Christ himself, the Good News of God, is the first and greatest evangelizer: "He has sent me to bring glad tidings to the poor" (Luke 4:18). Jesus' mission to proclaim the kingdom of God was the purpose of his Incarnation. A profound consciousness of this mission was ever present in his mind and heart.

Jesus proclaimed the kingdom of his Father untiringly and on every opportunity. He confirmed his authority to do so by countless signs and wonders; above all, by his death and Resurrection and the sending of the Holy Spirit upon the infant church.

At the very heart of his preaching was the Good News that God's great gift of salvation, promising liberation from everything that oppresses, is offered freely to everyone.

HIS CHURCH MUST ALSO EVANGELIZE

The Church of Jesus, the continuation of his presence and activity on earth, shares the very same mission from the Father. She exists to evangelize and to preach, to be a channel of graces won by Christ, to reconcile all persons to the Father. Evangelization flows from her very nature.

The church was born of the evangelizing activity of Jesus and the apostles.

The church was sent on her mission by Jesus, as he was sent by the Father. Each of the people of God should make his or her contribution to this mission.

The church, as the depository of the Good News, must preserve it as a precious living heritage and communicate it to all.

As evangelizer, the church must first internalize the Gospel by her own conversion and renewal in order to evangelize the world with credibility. Only then can she send out authentic evangelizers.

WHAT IS EVANGELIZATION

Evangelizing means bringing the Good News into every level of human society and through its influence transforming humankind from within. It has the human person as its starting point and human relationships as its concern as it tries to regenerate humanity through its encounter with the Gospel.

There is no true evangelization if the name, the teaching, the life, the promises, the kingdom and the mystery of Jesus of Nazareth, the Son of God, are not proclaimed.

The proclamation reaches full development when it is listened to, accepted, and assimilated and when it evokes genuine commitment in the one who has received it. This one enters a community which is, in itself, a sign of transformation—a sign of the newness of life: it is the church, the Sacrament of Salvation.

The Gospel must be proclaimed by the witness of the Christian life. Such a witness is a silent proclamation of the Good News, very powerful and very effective. All Christians are called to this witness and thus they become real evangelizers.

Evangelization then has varied elements: renewal of humanity through adherence to the Gospel, the witness of a Christian life, the explicit proclamation of the Good News, membership in a community of salvation, acceptance of signs, and apostolic initiative.

THE CONTENT OF EVANGELIZATION

The center of the message is the clear proclamation that in Jesus Christ, the Son of God made man, salvation is offered to every human being. The content of evangelization includes the following:

the prophetic proclamation of a hereafter.

the preaching of hope in God's promises.

the love of God and his love for us.

the love of the neighbor.

the mystery of evil and the search for good.

the search for God through prayer and the sacraments.

the rights and duties of every human being, of family life, life in society, and the promotion of peace and justice.

To evangelize is first of all to bear witness, in a simple and direct way, to God revealed by Jesus Christ in the Holy Spirit: to bear witness that in his son, God has loved the world—that in his incarnate Word he has given being to all things and has called every man and woman to eternal life.

One cannot promote the new commandment—to love one's neighbor—without promoting authentic human development. Evangelization must take the whole person into account, in all his aspects, including his openness to the absolute.

The church is becoming ever more conscious of the proper manner and the evangelical means she possesses to collaborate in the liberation of peoples. She is trying more and more to encourage large numbers of Christians to devote themselves to the liberation of human beings. And the necessity of ensuring fundamental human rights cannot be separated from liberation.

THE MISSION TO EVANGELIZE

Who has the mission to evangelize? By command of the Lord the whole church has the sacred duty to go out to the whole world and preach the Gospel to every creature. Evangelization is the basic duty of the people of God.

No evangelizer has sovereign control of the act of evangelization. He or she acts in communion with the church and its pastors. The individual churches have the task of assimilating the essence of the Gospel message and of transposing and proclaiming it in languages that people understand.

Christ's mandate to preach the Gospel is directed primarily to the bishops, in union with Peter; to priests who are associated with this ministry through ordination; to religious, whose lives are signs of their total availability to God, the church, and community; to the laity, who exercise a special form of evangelization in the world; to the family, "the domestic church," where the members evangelize one another; and to all others called to various ministries and endowed with special charisms by the Lord.

Because modern people listen more readily to witnesses than to teachers, the church will evangelize the world primarily by her conduct, by her living witness of faithfulness to the Lord Jesus.

The supreme importance of preaching must be emphasized because faith comes by hearing the word of God, which comes by preaching (Rom. 10:14f). Among the means to be used are the homily, catechetical instruction, and the powerful means of mass media.

Besides the collective proclamation of the Gospel, the person-to-person sharing of the Gospel is important. By this one shares the personal experience of his or her faith and thus touches individual consciences.

As the role of evangelization is to educate the faithful to live the sacramental life, evangelization will achieve its full development only when it achieves a permanent and unbroken union between Word and sacrament.

Thus we see that the divine mandate: "Go into the whole world and proclaim the good news to all creation" (Mark 16:15) is addressed to every Christian. The apostles and first-generation Christians understood this and made it into a program of action.

Today, twenty centuries later, each member of the church, the people of God, must do likewise. The Holy Spirit, the principal agent of evangelization, will inspire each one to proclaim the Gospel and will cause that proclamation to be understood and accepted. Evangelization was inaugurated on the first Pentecost and it must continue throughout the second one!

Questions to Ask Yourself

1. Are you really convinced that God has given you a mission to proclaim the Good News?

2. Does your present life give witness to the fact that Jesus Christ lived, suffered and died, and rose from the dead for you?

3. Do you live what you believe and do you preach what you live?

4. Are you trying to make Jesus Christ, the light of the world and the beloved of the Father, the king and center of your heart?

5. Do you believe that your work of evangelization will be as effective as your love of the evangelized?

CHAPTER XIV

SUMMARY

The opening sentence of this book quoted from the first encyclical of Pope John Paul II, in which he stated that Jesus Christ is the center of the human race and of history.

The paramount question for each of us to answer is: "Is he the center of my human life and of my history of personal salvation?"

Jesus Christ has called us to be his disciples and our personal relationship with him flows from this. We are invited to be his companions on a long and sometimes difficult journey. We should not be dismayed that the effort to understand and imitate him is a gradual process. It was no different with the original disciples.

After all, we are dealing with the most unique person in all of history. Reason, as well as God's revelation, leads to the conclusion that we must permit him to reveal himself to us in his own way and at his own time. Indeed, it is the

Father who reveals his beloved Son to us. And remember, the One who declared that he was the Way and the Truth and the Life also reassured us by saying: "I have called you friends."

Each of us, consciously or otherwise, operates out of a certain vision of life. This vision not only includes the goals we set for our lives —our entire system of values—but also embraces our habitual way of looking at all of life's events and the conscious and unconscious motivations in all that we seek or do.

Jesus' call to "Come and Follow Me" is more than an invitation to walk in the way he has shown us—it is an invitation to accept a totally renewed vision of life based on his Gospel. His ideal seems to be just another impossible dream, but only if we overlook the fact that he has promised to give us a new heart and a new spirit with which to achieve that dream. He seeks a wholehearted change from within— from the deepest core of our selfhood from which proceed all our desires, reflections, and motivations.

What the Lord means by conversion is that our make up and our lifestyle have to be brought into conformity with the will of our Father. This kind of conversion will always be a generous response to the person and the words of the Lord Jesus. He is the Good News par excellence and each new stage of growth implies a deeper blending of our lives with his. It quickly becomes obvious that this relationship is a dynamic, living business that embraces the totality of our lives. And there are no limits to the possible intimacy and depth of this relationship for the Christian.

A fundamental conviction underlying this relationship with the Lord should be the growing belief that he loves us totally and unconditionally at whatever stage of growth he finds us. Unfortunately our patterns of guilt frequently sabotage this conviction. Our response to the person of Jesus is best stimulated by the ever-deepening awareness of his unchanging and faithful love for us.

In the final judgment, the life story of each Christian is but the record of his or her personal relationship with the Lord. This relationship begins by looking at, listening to, and spending time with Christ, coupled with the willingness to let him refashion us in the likeness of the Father. On the Lord's part, we rely on his willingness to share all his gifts with us and his desire to share every aspect of our lives.

When we look to the apostles we discover that the chief characteristic of their spirituality was their personal relationship with Jesus.

Because they are our models in spirituality, we must expect to go through the same spiritual stages that they experienced. The commitment that radically changed their lives was their response to the person and words of Jesus. They formed communities of faith and hope, of love and concern who worked and prayed together to build up the body of Christ.

The apostles' vocation to preach the Gospel was but an opportunity to share their experience of Christ. They gave witness to his life and message by showing his impact on their own hearts and lives. We may relate best to the Apostle Paul because he, like us, knew only the risen Christ. He could sincerely state that "for me to live is Christ" because he had internalized the truth that Jesus *is* the power, and the wisdom, and the love of God Incarnate!

As the apostles grew in grace, they discovered that at the heart of the spirituality of Jesus was his profoundly intimate relationship with his Father—a relationship that he is eager to share with us.

The supreme value in the life of Jesus, as it should be in ours, was his ever-present and unconditional love of his Father as manifested in the unswerving performance of his will.

Jesus' life was simply one of loving service of his flock. He went about doing good and that goodness was the ultimate sign that God was among his people. This sign has never changed and wherever we witness a compassionate, healing, serving love we have the surest sign of the presence of God.

To become a spiritual person is increasingly to experience Jesus as the Lord of one's life. The essence of that life is how we relive the mystery of the life, death, and Resurrection of Jesus Christ, or what we call the Paschal Mystery. This ongoing, growing experience is the central fact in the life of each Christian. It calls for an openness to the presence of the Spirit of Jesus and a response to his work and action within us—eventually a total surrender of our life, our talents, and our energies to him.

Above all, it demands that the Lord be a part of all our relationships in life. It is our interaction with others—our imitation of Jesus—and our efforts to become a truly loving person that will engage us in a dying (to selfishness) and a rising (to godliness) process in which spiritual growth happens. And through all this, our special uniqueness, also a part of God's eternal plan, is to be preserved.

It is imperative that we, as disciples of Jesus, remain in conscious contact with the Master at each stage of our life and mission. This contact with the mind and heart of the Lord is impossible without frequent prayer. This personal communication with the Lord demands a conscious involvement of the whole person. As a person is, so does he or she pray—it is the total person that engages God in prayer.

Throughout this book, we have treated of the spiritual life as our unique response to God, ever revealing himself in the present moment. God is always breaking into our life through persons and events, through his Word and sacraments, through joy and sorrow, and, above all, through the person of his well-beloved Son Jesus. It is very difficult, if not impossible, to be alert and responsive to this inbreaking without the habitual communication we call prayer.

We shall soon discover that success or failure in prayer depends on our habitual orientation toward God, just as the type of prayer depends on the habitual image we have of the Lord. One thing is sure—we must spend time in this loving communication.

The Scriptures, above all, should be the nourishment of our prayer life because it is "through his living Word that God enters into contact with those he addresses revealing himself and manifesting the secrets of his inward life and love."

Through the sacraments we encounter the same Jesus that we read about and reflect upon in the pages of his Gospel. They are signs of his presence and love through which he offers forgiveness and peace, reconciliation and holiness. They are indeed needed to achieve the complete change of heart through which the Lord grants us a new heart and a new spirit that guarantee the spiritual renewal of our lives.

The Sacrament of Reconciliation (Penance) attempts to make visible in a joyful and thankful way God's healing action in our hearts and upon our person. It is a celebration of God's healing love and an effective sign of our reconciliation with God and humankind. It heals the selfishness that causes our alienation from God and man. Considering that spirituality always deals in relationships, we can quickly deduce the supreme importance of this sacrament in the effort to become truly a whole person.

Because "The Eucharist is the outstanding means whereby the faithful express in their lives and to others the mystery of Christ and the real nature of the church," this is the memorial par excellence of the life of Jesus —one that continues his incarnational presence, bringing with it his power, his love, and his companionship.

The basic effort of the Eucharistic celebration will always be to remember Jesus Christ. The Eucharist calls together the community of

Christ's faithful to remember the Lord in a way that perfectly glorifies the Father and opens us to his healing love. It invites all to union with the Heart of Jesus in love.

The sign above all others that stamps us with the authentic seal of a disciple of Christ will always be our charity. This healing, affirming, forgiving, serving love must become the significant quality of our lives: "By this will men know that you are my disciples." It is a love based not only on the command and the example of Christ, but also on a profound reverence for each human person who touches our lives.

Jesus spent a great deal of time with the unwanted and unloved and never seemed to be distressed by the thoughtlessness of those who demanded his time and attention. He wanted to remove from the lives of those that suffer anything that hurt them. His apostles were deeply touched by his compassionate concern.

He realized, with his deep knowledge of human nature, that only when a person is aware of being loved does he or she have the sense of self-worth needed to become free and secure. And the only way to free a person from feelings of self-alienation and self-rejection is to befriend and love that person. We simply do not grow as human beings or as Christians except in an environment of acceptance and support, of love and friendliness. Thus, we have an awesome responsibility to affirm the worth of every person we encounter. We may even be ourselves one of "the least of the brethren" and need special kindness and affirmation from ourselves!

In the pages of this book, the Christian life has been presented as a deep and growing relationship with the Lord Jesus, and through him with the Father and the Holy Spirit. The daily abiding in Christ—the special fruit of this relationship—not only gives a profound meaning to this life, it is also our claim to life eternal. As St. Paul writes: "Christ in you [is] your hope of glory."

Reading the signs of the times, I think every reflective person will agree that the faithful of Christ have been undergoing a profound purification in the years following Vatican II. This should not surprise anyone striving for a renewed life in Christ. The spiritual crises we have suffered are but a deeper sharing in the Passion of Jesus given by Divine Providence to prepare us for a greater manifestation of the presence of the risen Christ within us.

Our hope through it all is firmly based on the infallible promise of Jesus to be always with us. The Christian life is the life of Jesus within us, rooted in grace, and vibrant with faith, hope, and charity. He is our light, our friend, our way, our joy, and our Savior. Even though we may not be aware of it, not a moment passes that he does not present himself in the guise of some person, event, some light, some grace—yes, even at times of our worst temptations. He is truly risen and he is truly with us.

As we said at the beginning, there can be no evangelization, therefore, if the name, the life, the teaching, the promises, the kingdom, and the mystery of Jesus of Nazareth, the Son of God, are not proclaimed.

The mission of Jesus, as the first evangelizer, was to proclaim his Father's kingdom. At the heart of his preaching was the Good News that salvation, the great gift of God, offering liberation from everything that oppresses man, is offered to each of us as a free gift of God. He not only preached the Good News—he *is* the Good News!

We also evangelize not only by proclaiming Jesus Christ and his Way unceasingly, but also by giving witness—each in his or her own way —to his impact on our lives. The personal relationship with Jesus that we enjoy should simply overflow into every aspect of our lives. And then, we become, as did Jesus, *the Good News of God!*